The **Reflective Educator's Guide** to **Professional Development**

For all the outstanding and dedicated teacher inquirers we have had the opportunity to work with throughout our careers.

The **Reflective Educator's** **Guide** to **Professional Development**

Coaching Inquiry-Oriented Learning Communities

NANCY FICHTMAN DANA   DIANE YENDOL-HOPPEY

Foreword by Joellen Killion

A Joint Publication

 **CORWIN PRESS**
A SAGE Company
Thousand Oaks, CA 91320

For information:

Corwin Press
A SAGE Company
2455 Teller Road
Thousand Oaks, California 91320
www.corwinpress.com

SAGE India Pvt. Ltd.
B 1/I 1 Mohan Cooperative
    Industrial Area
Mathura Road, New Delhi 110 044
India

SAGE Ltd.
1 Oliver's Yard
55 City Road
London EC1Y 1SP
United Kingdom

SAGE Asia-Pacific Pte. Ltd.
33 Pekin Street #02-01
Far East Square
Singapore 048763

Printed in the United States of America.

Library of Congress Cataloging-in-Publication Data

Dana, Nancy Fichtman, 1964-
The reflective educator's guide to professional development: Coaching inquiry-oriented learning communities/Nancy Fichtman Dana, Diane Yendol-Hoppey.
     p. cm.
"A joint publication with the National Staff Development Council."
Includes bibliographical references and index.
ISBN 978-1-4129-5579-9 (cloth)
ISBN 978-1-4129-5580-5 (pbk.)
    1. Teachers—In-service training. 2. Teachers—Professional relationships. 3. Action research in education. I. Yendol-Silva, Diane. II. Title.

LB1731.D35 2008
370.71'5—dc22   2007045637

This book is printed on acid-free paper.

08   09   10   11   12   10   9   8   7   6   5   4   3   2

Acquisitions Editor:	Carol Collins
Editorial Assistant:	Brett Ory
Production Editor:	Jenn Reese
Copy Editor:	Trey Thoelcke
Typesetter:	C&M Digitals (P) Ltd.
Proofreader:	Victoria Reed-Castro
Indexer:	Ellen Slavitz
Cover Designer:	Michael Dubowe
Graphic Designer:	Lisa Riley

Contents

List of Figures

Foreword

Improving teaching and student learning requires intensive focus on refining the interaction between teachers and students in classrooms. Professional development holds the potential for dramatically improving teaching and student learning. Yet not all professional development produces such lofty results. For some teachers, professional development is more torture than treasure.

Menu-driven professional development models, while offering multiple opportunities for teacher learning, fail to create a laserlike focus on what happens each day in classrooms. This kind of focus results from professional development that occurs daily as a regular part of teachers' workday, focuses on the content they teach and their school's goals for improvement, expands their pedagogy, deepens their content knowledge, and engages them in professional collaboration with their colleagues. This kind of professional development builds collective responsibility among a school staff for student success and shifts the culture within the school so that everyone learns every day. This type of professional learning requires developing the capacity of professional development leaders in each school who serve as learning facilitators.

A learning facilitator orchestrates, supports, organizes, leads, or guides the learning among educators. As one of the ten roles of coaches (Killion & Harrison, 2006), a learning facilitator understands how to structure learning experiences that allow teachers to learn with and from each other in productive and efficient ways. In many schools, learning facilitators are coaches who work to enhance teaching.

Coaches are frequently master teachers who work in a single or multiple schools. They may also be district-based staff, school- or district-based administrators, or external assistance providers who provide classroom- and school-based support to improve instruction, content knowledge, leadership, and student learning.

The Reflective Educator's Guide to Professional Development: Coaching Inquiry-Oriented Learning Communities offers support for learning facilitators as they engage teachers in collaborative action research. Dana and Yendol-Hoppey drill deeply into the action research process to offer coaching strategies that amplify teachers' learning at each stage of the process and build a community of professionals.

The authors draw on their extensive experience with action research, professional learning communities, and coaching to provide guidance on shaping a culture of inquiry, building trust and safe places for risk taking, reflection, and revision. They offer new insights on action research and demonstrate how coaching promotes learning at each step of the process. They share examples of interactions between coaches and teachers to model skillful questioning, laserlike focus, and authentic inquiry. Each chapter is filled with useful and easy-to-access tools that coaches can use in their work.

The authors' most valuable contribution may be their insight on how to generate opportunities for productive collaboration in learning communities focused on deep reflection and inquiry on practice and learning. Within these collaborative interactions, teacher expertise emerges and contributes to student learning. Dana and Yendol-Hoppey are clear that when teachers collaborate about their practice and engage in inquiry using action research, there are two beneficiaries—teachers' professionalism and students' academic success.

—Joellen Killion

Deputy Executive Director of the
National Staff Development Council

Preface

Throughout the years, those responsible for the professional learning of teachers have come to realize that a great deal of untapped knowledge about teaching and learning resides within the schoolhouse itself (Killion & Harrison, 2006). The delivery of effective professional development has transitioned from the sole provision of in-service days where students have a holiday and teachers come to work to listen to an outside expert share knowledge about a new educational innovation to tapping the greatest underutilized source of knowledge about teaching and learning that exists within a school—the teachers and principals who work there! Two ways teacher and principal knowledge has been accessed to provide meaningful and powerful professional development are through *professional learning communities* (PLCs) and *action research*. These two mechanisms for professional development have literally exploded across the nation, as hundreds of school districts realize the potential school-based professional development holds for teacher growth and learning.

While both PLCs and action research hold tremendous potential for improving the teaching and learning that occurs in schools and have become a rampant form of professional development across the nation, the quality of the PLC and action research experience, and therefore the success these experiences hold for reforming schools, is directly related to the quality of the coaching teachers engaged in this work receive. Yet, there exists little literature on the coaching process.

- What makes an effective coach?
- What activities and tools do coaches use to spur the professional development of the teachers with whom they work?
- How do coaches make decisions about what activities and tools to use and when to use them?
- How can two of the most popular forms of school-based professional development (PLCs and action research) be combined so that they can enhance each other, and therefore, magnify the already powerful professional development practices occurring in many schools and districts across the nation?

This book was written to provide answers to these questions and to support those who work in teacher professional development—district and school-based staff developers, grade- and department-level team leaders, coaches, principals, mentor teachers, teacher-leaders, educational consultants, and university professors—in the awesome responsibility of facilitating the professional growth and learning of others. Whether you have established PLCs or action research in your school, or are interested in beginning this work, this book can help you think about the many nuances that exist in leading school-based professional development or enhance the systems you already have in place. In addition, courses in action research are common at the university level as professors assist teachers working on advanced degrees discover the power of studying their own practice in a systematic way or induct novice teachers into the teaching profession as lifelong learners and inquirers. This book can also be useful for university professors who teach these courses, to provide ideas for how to structure your course as a PLC with action research becoming the product of structuring your course in this way.

There is no job that is more important than coaching the professional development of teachers. Yet, for years, the act of coaching has not been made explicit. There exists a plethora of books on action research and PLCs, but few link together these two concepts that have so much in common, and so much to offer each other. Furthermore, few are the resources that make the action of coaching and the actions coaches take explicit. Those who coach professional development are often left on their own to decipher the many materials on how to do action research and what constitutes a PLC, and figure out for themselves what it means to coach these processes. We became amazed that so few resources existed to help coaches do what they do best—support the learning and growth of teachers. Therefore, we wrote this book to make explicit what we have learned based on our own experiences coaching school-based professional development ourselves, as well as research we have conducted on this process for almost twenty years. Over this period, we have had the honor of working with many incredible coaches, and share many of their stories and practices in this book in an effort to make the work of the coach visible for all.

ABOUT THIS BOOK

To make the work of coaching school-based professional development explicit, we begin in Chapter 1 by discussing the question, "What constitutes powerful professional development?" We then provide brief synopses of two processes that meet the criteria for powerful professional development—action research and PLCs. We end the first chapter by comparing these two processes, noting commonalities and suggesting how action research and PLCs can combine into a new entity—inquiry-oriented PLCs. We define inquiry-oriented PLCs as a group of six to twelve professionals who meet on a regular basis to learn from practice through structured dialogue and engage in continuous cycles through the process of action research (articulating a wondering, collecting data to gain insights into the wondering, analyzing data, making improvements in practice based on what was learned, and sharing learning with others).

In Chapter 2, we discuss the finer points of establishing and maintaining an inquiry-oriented PLC, and what is needed logistically to ensure that the building blocks for a healthy and successful PLC are in place. If you are just beginning as a coach, this chapter will provide many ideas for organizing and calling the initial meetings of your PLC. If you are currently coaching an existing PLC, this chapter will help you review and assess the essential elements of a healthy and high-functioning PLC, and plan meeting(s) to address areas in your PLC that may need attention. Specifically, in this chapter, we share protocols and stories to establish effective ground rules for gatherings, enforce ground rules by identifying behaviors consistent and inconsistent with them, enable colleagues to develop the trust necessary to share information freely with each other, help them attend fully to each other's perspective, and make a collective commitment to the process of action research (J. P. McDonald, Mohr, Dichter, & McDonald, 2003).

To help you develop a vision for how the process of action research can be intricately intertwined with the work of a new or established PLC, in the next four chapters of this book we explore four critical junctures in the action research process in depth, sharing our own stories as well as the stories of many excellent inquiry-oriented PLC coaches we have observed in action, as they facilitate group members' development of questions or wonderings for study (Chapter 3), help teachers develop an action research plan (Chapter 4), assist teachers as they analyze their data (Chapter 5), and provide spaces for teachers to share their inquiry work with others (Chapter 6). Embedded in each of these chapters are numerous examples of specific strategies, activities, and tools you can use in your own coaching work, as well as an articulation of the thinking that went into each action the coaches took as their work facilitating inquiry-oriented PLCs unfolded throughout the school year. Finally, in Chapter 7, we share one dozen "Lessons Learned" about coaching inquiry-oriented PLCs compiled from the various coaches of teacher professional development we have worked with throughout the years.

In whatever role you play in facilitating and supporting the professional growth of teachers, we hope this text provides helpful ideas for you to consider as you lead renewal and reform efforts from within the four walls of your school or district. Happy Inquiring!

Acknowledgments

Throughout our careers, we have had the honor and privilege to work with many tremendous educators that had taken on the responsibility of facilitating the professional growth and learning of teachers—teacher-leaders, mentor teachers, district staff developers, coaches, and principals. Throughout our careers, we have also always been passionate about raising the voices of practitioners in educational reform, teaching, and teacher education. In an effort to raise practitioner voices, we weave within this text many rich examples and stories of the educators we have witnessed engaged in masterful coaching of teacher professional development. Hence, this book would not have been possible without the stories and practices provided by these teachers and administrators.

In particular, we wish to name Broward County Professional Development Coach extraordinaire, Terry Campenella; Miami-Dade School District magnificent National School Reform Faculty Members, Pete Bermudez and Linda Emm; Alachua Elementary School's terrific Teacher Leader, Kevin Berry; University of Florida's wonderful Professional Development School Coordinator, Darby Delane; and the North East Florida Educational Consortium's fabulous Inquiry Facilitators: Rhonda Clyatt, Leanne Criscitiello, Anna Faulconer, Debbi Hubbell, Jack Hughes, Sherri Jackson, John Kreinbihl, Lynn Marshall, Mickey MacDonald, Cindy McCray, Tracie Snow, Kim Sullivan, Tracy Taylor, and Joan Thate.

In addition to these practitioners, we are fortunate to work with the phenomenal staff and faculty at one of the few remaining University Lab Schools in the nation—P.K. Yonge Developmental Research School. We wish to thank P.K. Yonge Director, Fran Vandiver, who continually both supports and pushes our thinking about inquiry work as well as all of the teachers at P.K. who have engaged in inquiry-oriented PLC work with us throughout the years.

In addition to these extraordinary teachers and coaches of teacher professional development, we are grateful to a number of principals who have engaged in inquiry-oriented PLC work with us. We have learned a great deal about making inquiry a part of staff development practice rather than an add-on to teachers' already full plates through the work and support of the following principals: Jim Brandenburg, Mark Bracewell, Teri Buckles, Ann Hayes, Lynette Langford, and Marion McCray.

We would also like to acknowledge the important multiyear research initiative, "The Peer Collaboration Initiative," conducted by a team led by Dr. Betty Lou Whitford and funded by the Lucent Technologies Foundation. This project aimed at developing PLCs in K–12 schools and the research from this initiative significantly informed this book, as well as encouraged us to share the nuts and bolts of inquiry-oriented PLC work with those coaching the work in schools. We are particularly grateful to Diane Wood, Hallie Tamez, and Debra Smith for their important work, mentoring, and friendship.

In addition, The North East Florida Educational Consortium (NEFEC) has provided invaluable support for inquiry-oriented PLC work to take root in sixteen districts in North-Central Florida. We are grateful to NEFEC's Sabrina Crosby, Bob Smith, Marsha Hill, Ashley McCool, and Jason Arnold for their support and for their passion for providing powerful professional development to the districts with whom they work.

We also wish to thank a number of people at the University of Florida. Chris Sessums, Distance Education Director, provided assistance in the construction of stories used in this text that were related to the integration of technology into instruction. Katie Tricarico, Graduate Research Assistant for the Center for School Improvement, helped to create some of the figures for this text. Susan Stabel, Senior Secretary for the Center for School Improvement at UF, provided assistance in the preparation of this manuscript. Colleagues in the Lastinger Center for Learning—Don Pemberton, Alyson Adams, and Sylvia Boynton—provided wonderful feedback in our development of this model for inquiry-oriented PLCs as they applied these concepts to their work in high-need, high-poverty schools across the state of Florida. In addition to our colleagues at University of Florida, we thank the wonderful acquisitions editors and editorial assistants at Corwin Press—Carol Collins, Faye Zucker, Brett Ory, and Gem Rabanera, who all helped this book move from conceptualization to reality.

Finally, we wish to thank our husbands, Tom Dana (Director, School of Teaching and Learning at University of Florida), and David Hoppey (Inclusion Supervisor for the Alachua County Schools). These men continue to be our closest colleagues and best friends! We also wish to thank our children, Greg, Kirsten, Caran, Billy, and Kevin, whose experiences in schools continue to fuel our passion to keep inquiry alive for teachers and the children they teach. Without our family's loving support and consultation, this book could not have been written.

Corwin Press would like to thank the following individuals for their contributions:

Amy Allen, Educational Consultant, Baton Rouge, LA

Roland Barth, Educator and Author, Alna, ME

Terry A. Crawley, Coordinator for School Planning and Professional Development, Archdiocese of Louisville, Louisville, KY

Kathy Malnar, Superintendent, Hudson Area Schools, Hudson, MI

Ellen Meyers, Senior Vice President, Teachers Network, New York, NY

Bill Osman, Supervisor of Professional Development and Mentoring, Hamilton Township Public Schools, Hamilton Twp., NJ

Gail Ritchie, Instructional Coach, Co-Leader Teacher Researcher Network, Fairfax County Public Schools, Burke, VA

Gina Segobiano, Superintendent, Harmony Emge School District #175, National Distinguished Principal, 2002, Belleville, IL

About the Authors

 **Nancy Fichtman Dana** is a Professor of Education and Director of the Center for School Improvement at the University of Florida (http://education.ufl.edu/csi). Under her direction, the center promotes and supports practitioner inquiry (action research) as a core mechanism for school improvement in schools throughout the state. She began her career in education as an elementary school teacher in Hannibal Central Schools, New York, and has worked closely with teachers and administrators on action research, building professional learning communities, and school-university collaborations in Florida and Pennsylvania since 1990. She has authored numerous articles in professional journals focused on teacher inquiry, as well as a bestselling book (with Diane Yendol-Hoppey) from Corwin Press on the action research process—*The Reflective Educator's Guide to Classroom Research*. Nancy Dana may be reached via e-mail at ndana@coe.ufl.edu.

 **Diane Yendol-Hoppey** is an Associate Professor in the School of Teaching and Learning at the University of Florida. She spent the first thirteen years of her career in education teaching in a variety of public schools in Pennsylvania and Maryland. Since joining the faculty at University of Florida in the autumn of 2000, her work with schools has focused on job-embedded, context sensitive teacher learning and the cultivation of teacher leadership. Her research explores how powerful vehicles for teacher professional development including teacher inquiry, professional learning communities, and coaching/mentoring can support school improvement. Her research has appeared in such journals as *Teachers College Record* and *Journal of Teacher Education*. She is coauthor (with Nancy Fichtman Dana) of two books, *The Reflective Educator's Guide to Classroom Research* and *The Reflective Educator's Guide to Mentoring*, both from Corwin Press. Diane Yendol-Hoppey may be reached via e-mail at dyhoppey@coe.ufl.edu.

1

Facilitating the Professional Development of Others

The Role of Action Research and Professional Learning Communities

> *Nothing within a school has more impact upon students in terms of skills development, self-confidence, or classroom behavior than the personal and professional growth of their teachers. When teachers examine, question, reflect on their ideas and develop new practices that lead towards their ideals, students are alive. When teachers stop growing, so do their students.*[1] *(Barth, 1981, p. 145)*

In the position of district or school-based staff developer, coach, principal, mentor, or teacher-leader, you have been charged with the awesome responsibility of facilitating the learning and professional growth of the teachers in your school and/or district. The job of keeping teachers alive and growing throughout their careers is more important than ever! Given the pressures of high-stakes testing and national, state, and district mandates, coupled with the charge to meet the endless list of student needs, teachers are leaving the profession in record numbers (Luekens, Lyter, Fox, & Chandler, 2004). Those that remain are hungry for support as they strive to meet the endless challenges of teaching in today's schools. In your role of staff developer, coach, principal, or teacher-leader, you are uniquely positioned to fulfill the professional development appetites of teachers in your building, keeping them in the profession, and most importantly, keeping them vibrant and alive in their work. Staff developers who keep teachers vibrant and alive in their work also keep learning vibrant and alive for students each school day.

WHAT CONSTITUTES POWERFUL PROFESSIONAL DEVELOPMENT?

So what is the best way to nourish the professional development of teachers? In the past fifty years, we have learned a great deal about what powerful professional development does and does not look like. Historically, the most prominent model of professional development has taken the form of workshops delivered on in-service days when teachers work, but students have a holiday (Cochran-Smith & Lytle, 1999a). In these workshops, sometimes referred to as "sit and get" professional development, teachers often learn about a new pedagogy from an outside expert, and then go back to their classrooms the next school day to implement the new knowledge that was handed down from the expert. This type of training emphasizes developing a certain type of knowledge, referred to by Cochran-Smith and Lytle (1999a) as knowledge *for* practice.

Knowledge *for* practice is often reflected in traditional professional development efforts when a trainer shares with teachers information produced by educational researchers. This knowledge presumes a level of correctness about specific teaching practices based on conventional scientific methods that "yields a commonly accepted degree of significance, validity, generalizability, and intersubjectivity" (Cochran-Smith & Lytle, 1999a, p. 255, referencing Fenstermacher, 1994, p. 8). Given that research can wisely inform teaching practice, this knowledge *for* practice, often generated and shared by an outside source, is useful to teacher growth but not sufficient. Knowledge *for* practice may suggest a potential solution for a generic learning dilemma but offers little insight into how to implement that solution within the teacher's specific classroom context. In most cases, teachers need support as they transfer that newly acquired knowledge to the learning process within their classrooms. The problem with relying solely on professional development focused on knowledge *for* practice is that these researched-based practices are not necessarily easily transferable to a specific classroom context.

Therefore, experienced educators know that knowledge *for* practice as the sole focus of professional development may be an efficient method of disseminating information, but often does not satisfy teachers' yearning for meaningful professional development or result in real and meaningful change in the classroom. After a workshop, teachers often return to their classrooms without support to implement the new knowledge they gained as a result of workshop participation, and anything that may have been good or useful about the workshop often gets lost in the already established daily routines, pressures, and isolation of teaching. In addition, this model of professional development relies solely on the expertise of educators outside of the school and/or district. In many cases, the expertise of a district's own teaching force is never acknowledged or shared. Finally, this model of professional development does not acknowledge the tremendous complexities inherent in teaching.

Translating new strategies, approaches, and pedagogy from theory to practice within individual classrooms is rarely a simple task for teachers, and it is natural for dilemmas to emerge when implementing an innovation. The traditional model of professional development offers no mechanism to help teachers understand and address these dilemmas that emerge as they implement new practices within their classrooms. Thus, educators involved with the professional development of teachers must also cultivate knowledge *in* practice.

Knowledge *in* practice recognizes the importance of teacher practical knowledge and its role in improving teaching practice. Often this type of knowledge is generated as teachers begin testing out their new knowledge for practice gained from traditional professional development training. As teachers apply this new knowledge, they construct knowledge *in* practice by engaging in their daily work within their classroom and school. Knowledge *in* practice is strengthened as teachers deliberatively reflect about specific teaching episodes and articulate the tacit knowledge embedded in their experiences. Knowledge *in* practice is strengthened through collaboration with peers. Professional development vehicles, including mentoring and peer coaching, rely on collaboration and dialogue that can generate reflection as well as make public the new knowledge being created.

A third type of knowledge that is gaining attention from professional developers today is knowledge *of* practice. Knowledge *of* practice stresses that through systematic inquiry "teachers make problematic their own knowledge and practice as well as the knowledge and practice of others" (Cochran-Smith & Lytle, 1999a, p. 273). Teachers create this kind of knowledge as they focus on raising questions about and systematically studying their own classroom teaching. Cochran-Smith and Lytle suggest that "what goes on inside the classroom is profoundly altered and ultimately transformed when teachers' frameworks for practice foreground the intellectual, social, and cultural contexts of teaching" (p. 276). What this means is that as teachers engage in this type of knowledge construction, they move beyond the "nuts and bolts" of classroom practice to examine how these "nuts and bolts" might reflect larger social structures and roles that could potentially inhibit student learning. Teachers interested in constructing knowledge *of* practice receive support as they collaboratively inquire with colleagues about how their own teaching practices might inhibit the learning that takes place in their schools and classrooms. For example, teachers might work in study groups to uncover hidden agendas and explore issues of race, class, gender, culture, language, or ability that might influence the learning within their school and classrooms.

Dissatisfied with the traditional "sit and get" model of professional development, scholars throughout the past several decades have suggested the need for new approaches to professional development that acknowledge all three types of teacher knowledge. By attending to developing knowledge *for, in,* and *of* practice, we can enhance professional growth that leads to real change. Figure 1.1 outlines the three different types of teacher knowledge that we have shared as important to those striving to support teacher learning, as well as some of the professional development activities that can cultivate that type of knowledge.

Borne out of the dialogue focused on developing all three types of teacher knowledge and moving away from relying on the traditional "sit and get" professional development model, two driving forces for meaningful, powerful professional development have gained momentum in schools throughout the nation: action research and PLCs.

WHAT IS ACTION RESEARCH?

Action research, also referred to as teacher research, teacher inquiry, or practitioner inquiry, is defined as systematic, intentional study by teachers of their own classroom practice (Cochran-Smith & Lytle, 1993). Action researchers seek out change and reflect on their practice by posing questions or "wonderings," collecting data to gain insights into their wonderings, analyzing the data along with reading relevant literature, making changes in practice based on new understandings developed during inquiry, and sharing findings with others (Dana & Yendol-Silva, 2003).

Example: A Fourth Grade Teacher Researches Reading Fluency

To illustrate the process of action research, we turn to teacher-researcher Debbi Hubbell. Debbi teaches fourth grade in a rural elementary school located in North Florida. Intrigued when her principal offered the opportunity

Figure 1.1 Types of Teacher Knowledge and Professional Development

	Knowledge for Practice	*Knowledge* in Practice	*Knowledge* of Practice
Knowledge Source	Knowledge that is the result of generalizable behaviors and techniques that show potential and are verified and acknowledged as effective.	Knowledge that recognizes the importance of teacher practical knowledge and its role in improving teaching practice.	Knowledge that emerges from teacher questions about their practice and results from the systematic study of their classroom teaching.
Professional Development Activities	Read a professional book or journal.	Implement an innovation and reflect individually.	Engage in teacher research individually.
	Attend a workshop or professional meeting.	Implement an innovation and reflect with a mentor or peer coach.	Engage in teacher research with a partner.
	Participate in a book club.	Implement an innovation and reflect within a learning community.	Engage in teacher research as a part of a learning community.
	Observe another teacher.	Engage in teacher research around a particular innovation.	
		Engage in Japanese Lesson Study.	

to engage in teacher research as a part of staff development at her building, Debbi decided to look closely at one of her teaching passions—reading. Debbi knew that one of the best predictors of performance on Florida's yearly standardized test, the FCAT (Florida Comprehensive Assessment Test), was reading fluency, and that research has shown a direct correlation between fluency and comprehension. She wanted to help her students become more successful readers, and she believed that if they became more fluent they would develop their reading comprehension. In the end, this would also allow them to perform better on the FCAT.

Worried about seven students she felt were at risk and less fluent than others in her class, she decided to explore in more detail the research related to developing fluency in elementary readers. She attended numerous workshops and read a variety of research-based articles that developed her knowledge of fluency. As a result of this knowledge development, Debbie introduced the rereading of fractured fairy tale plays to these seven learners to see if this activity might increase reading fluency. The fractured fairy tales differed from the more traditional skill-and-drill activity these students often encountered in daily reading instruction.

To gain insights into her wondering, "What is the relationship between my fourth graders' fluency development and the reading of fractured fairy tale plays?" Debbi collected three forms of data. First, Debbi administered Dynamic Indicators of Basic Early Literacy Skills (DIBELS) at different times throughout her research. The DIBELS are a set of standardized, individually administered measures of early literacy development. They are designed to be short, one-minute fluency measures used to regularly monitor the development of prereading and early reading skills.

In addition, Debbi took anecdotal notes each time she utilized fractured fairy tale plays with these fourth grade students, documenting their reactions, engagement, and Debbi's assessment of their fluency development with each rereading of a play. Finally, Debbi relied on student work or artifacts as a third data source. At the end of the fractured fairy tale series, Debbi asked her students to write "Dear Mrs. Hubbell" letters, telling her about their perceptions and experiences with the fractured fairy tale unit of study.

Debbi analyzed her data by charting student DIBELS scores over time, as well as organizing and reading through her anecdotal notes and student-produced artifacts. Based on her data, Debbi could make three statements that characterized the knowledge *in* practice that she learned as a result of her research. First, all students' DIBELS scores improved over time. Second, the reading of fractured fairy tale plays generated enthusiasm for school and learning. A student who had hated school and was failing actually said later he enjoyed reading fractured fairy tales and producing them as a play. This student improved at least by a grade or more in *each* subject. Third, positive social interactions occurred between students who previously had difficulty communicating in a positive way. Students enjoyed helping each other when someone made a mistake in word recognition, stress, pitch, or phrasing, and tolerance, as well as admiration, replaced existing adversarial student-to-student relationships.

As her action research progressed, Debbi's data indicated the academic, social, and emotional value of fractured fairy tales. As a result, Debbi decided to move beyond the seven initial learners in her study to implement fractured fairy tales with her entire class. At the close of the school year, Debbi shared what she learned about the relationship between the reading of fractured fairy tale plays and the fluency development of her struggling fourth grade readers at a local action research conference. During the presentation she shared the academic, social, and emotional value of this strategy, as well as how her teaching changed as a result of this inquiry. She also received solid feedback on her inquiry from other teachers (Hubbell, 2005). Next, Debbie shared her research at a faculty meeting in her school. Her inquiry served as the impetus for her school to develop schoolwide fluency objectives and engage in dialogue to assess existing reading practices in her school and district.

WHAT ARE PLCs?

PLCs serve to connect and network groups of professionals to do just what their name entails—*learn* from practice. PLCs meet on a regular basis and their time together is often structured by the use of protocols to ensure focused, deliberate conversation and dialogue by teachers about student work and student learning. Joseph McDonald and his colleagues explain the importance of using protocols:

> In diplomacy, protocol governs who greets whom first when the President and Prime Minister meet, and other such matters. In technology, protocols enable machines to "talk" with one another by precisely defining the language they use. In science and medicine, protocols are regimens that ensure faithful replication of an experiment or treatment; they tell the scientist or doctor to do this first, then that, and so on. And in social science, they are the scripted questions that an interviewer covers, or the template for an observation. But in the professional education of educators? One could argue that elaborate etiquette, communicative precision, faithful replication, and scripts would prove counterproductive here. Don't we best learn from each other by just talking with each other? No, we claim. Among educators especially, *just* talking may not be enough. The kind of talking needed to educate ourselves cannot rise spontaneously and unaided from *just* talking. It needs to be carefully planned and scaffolded. (J. P. McDonald et al., 2003, p. 4)

Protocols for educators provide a script or series of timed steps for how a conversation among teachers on a chosen topic will develop.

A variety of different protocols have been developed for use in PLCs by a number of noteworthy organizations such as the National Staff Development Council (see, for example, Lois Brown Easton's *Powerful Designs for Professional Learning*) and the National School Reform Faculty (NSRF), who developed one version of a PLC called Critical Friends Groups (CFGs; NSRF, 2007). In its work conceptualizing CFGs, the NSRF laid much of the ground work for shifting the nature of the dialogue that occurs between and among teachers about their practice in schools, and is responsible for training thousands of teachers to focus on developing collegial relationships, encouraging reflective practice, and rethinking leadership in restructuring schools. Because of the intense focus and scope of the

NSRF's work, in this book we rely most heavily on resources developed by the NSRF. Further information about NSRF and access to their protocols can be found at http://www.nsrfharmony.org.

The CFGs provide deliberate time and structures dedicated to promoting adult professional growth that is directly linked to student learning. When used within a PLC, protocols ensure planned, intentional conversation by teachers about student work, a teacher's dilemma, a lesson to be taught, or other aspects of practice. Different protocols are selected for use depending on the topic for discussion that day.

Example: An Elementary School PLC Focuses on Inclusion

To illustrate the process of PLCs, we turn to the teachers in an elementary school in south Florida who were collectively struggling with how to survive the pressures of high-stakes testing and accountability. The teachers at Everglades Elementary School met for one or two hours at least twice a month during a designated shared planning time. A facilitator, who was the school's reading coach, led the group, which typically consisted of ten to twelve regular participants. The facilitator or coach would begin by stating the goals for the meeting, which had been set at the previous meeting. For example, the coach might state, "At our last meeting, we decided to look more closely at a concern of ours—inclusion."

To accomplish the goal of this meeting, the group read a short article that illustrated the importance of inclusion. After reading the short article, the group members used an NSRF protocol called "The 4As" to structure the text discussion. As group members read the article on inclusion, they highlighted and wrote notes in the margin to answer the following four questions:

1. What *assumptions* does the author of the text hold?

2. What do you *agree* with in the text?

3. What do you want to *argue* with in the text?

4. To what parts of the text do you want to *aspire*?

In a round, each person identified one assumption in the inclusion article, citing the article, with page numbers, as evidence. The group continued in rounds talking about the text in light of each remaining A, taking them one at a time—what do people want to argue with, agree with, and aspire to in the article. At the end of all four rounds, the coach led a general discussion focused on the question, "What does this mean for our work with students?" As a result of the reading and structured dialogue, the group deepened its understanding of inclusion. Upon concluding the discussion, the group debriefed the activity by identifying how members might improve the discussion in the future. At the end of the meeting, the facilitator led the group in establishing the goals for the next meeting.

Although the activity of the learning community might change, this same sequence is followed during each meeting. For example, in the next meeting the facilitator asked Cheryl, a group member, to share a dilemma of practice as the key activity of the group. This conversation focused on Cheryl's dilemma related to her students' work. The group helped her investigate "How do I improve the narrative writing of my students?" This discussion used an NSRF protocol called the "Collaborative Assessment Conference" to explore her students' writing, which she brought as "data" for the group to review.

Following the steps of this protocol, Cheryl passed out copies of her selected student's writing to the other members of the group. She said nothing about the work, the context in which it was created, or the student. The group members read the work in silence, making brief notes about aspects of it that were particularly striking to them.

In Step 2 of the protocol, called "Describing the Work," the facilitator asked the group, "What do you see?" Group members provided answers without making judgments about the quality of the work. If a judgment emerged, the facilitator asked for the evidence on which the judgment was based.

In Step 3, "Asking Questions about the Work," the facilitator asked the group, "What questions does this work raise for you?" Group members stated questions they had about the work, the child, the assignment, and the circumstances under which the work was created.

In Step 4, "Speculating," the facilitator asked the group, "What do you think the child is working on?" Group members made suggestions about the problems or issues that the student might have been focused on in carrying out the assignment. During Steps 3, 4, and 5, Cheryl listened carefully while also taking notes, but in following the rules of the protocol was not allowed to respond.

In Step 5, the facilitator invited Cheryl to speak about her perspective on the student's work, describing what she saw in it, responding to one or more of the questions raised, and adding any other information she thought was important for the group to know. Cheryl also commented on the surprising and unexpected things that she heard during the describing, questioning, and speculating steps of the protocol. Included in her comments was her emerging appreciation for more specifically developed rubrics as well as ideas for leading focused individual writing conferences during the school day.

In the final steps of the protocol, the facilitator invited members to share any thoughts they had about their own teaching, children's learning, or ways to support this particular child in the future. The protocol discussion ended with the group reflecting on the Collaborative Assessment Conference protocol and thanking Cheryl, the presenting teacher, for sharing the work of her student and her teaching dilemma.

At the end of this PLC meeting, the facilitator once again led the group in establishing the goal(s) for the next meeting. PLC meetings, characterized by this same sequence of events (the statement of the agreed-upon goal for the meeting, the selection and implementation of a protocol to guide discussion to accomplish the meeting goal, and the setting of the goal for the next meeting), continue as the PLC meets throughout the school year.

HOW CAN ACTION RESEARCH AND PLCs BECOME THE DYNAMIC DUO?

Action research and PLCs as mechanisms for teacher professional growth have a lot in common. Perhaps the most important, core, shared characteristic of action research and PLCs is the foundation on which each of these mechanisms for professional development is built. Both action research and PLCs acknowledge the overwhelming, inherent complexity of teaching and the multiple types of knowledge that teachers must create in order to change their teaching practices in ways that benefit all children.

To illustrate the complexity of teaching, let's talk for a moment about what it means to be a teacher. Effective teachers must know their content deeply, know pedagogy, know human development, know the 25 (in elementary school) to more than 100 (in secondary schools) students they interact with each day, including identifying each one of these learners' academic, social, and emotional needs, and teachers must attend to these individuals' needs, all unique and varied, all at the same time during each instructional moment of the day.

Teachers must understand lesson planning, and understand that with every lesson taught there will be a unique outcome that results from the interaction of the context of the teaching, the timing of the teaching, the teacher, and the learners in the room. Teachers must attend to management and transitions of large groups of learners before, during, and after each lesson. Teachers are bombarded with decision making each minute of their day, ranging from deciding the next steps when a planned lesson is not progressing productively to deciding if Jordan, who just asked to use the bathroom for the third time that day, should be given permission to leave the lesson to take care of his personal needs. In addition, teachers must constantly assess their students' learning, formally and informally.

Teachers also make contributions to the school by managing such tasks as lunch money collection, lunch counts, and bus and lunch duties. They must communicate and collaborate with parents as well as other education professionals, such as guidance counselors, the principal, school psychologists, and teaching colleagues. In their spare time, they serve on committees, attend faculty meetings, and read professional journals and books to keep abreast of the latest developments in their field. They do all of this while simultaneously keeping an eye on high-stakes testing and their students' performance, balancing preparation for test taking and the teaching of test-taking skills with real teaching and learning of content.

Both action research and PLCs, as mechanisms for teacher professional development, acknowledge the inherent complexity of teaching by embracing the notion that it is natural and normal for teachers to face many problems, issues, tensions, and dilemmas as they teach. Rather than sweeping the problems under the carpet and pretending they don't exist, teachers who conduct action research or become members of PLCs welcome problems by deliberately naming them, making them public, examining them, and making a commitment to do something about them.

Through both engagement in action research and PLC membership, questioning practice becomes part of the teacher's work, and eventually a part of the teaching culture. Both teacher research and PLCs are actualizations of an inquiry stance toward teaching that leads to job-embedded teacher knowledge construction. According to distinguished educational scholars Marilyn Cochran-Smith and Susan Lytle (2001):

> A legitimate and essential purpose of professional development is the development of an inquiry stance on teaching that is critical and transformative, a stance linked not only to high standards for the learning of all students but also to social change and social justice and to the individual and collective professional growth of teachers. (p. 46)

While teacher research and PLCs are prevalent and powerful mechanisms for enacting an inquiry stance toward teaching, many times they exist and operate independently of one another. We believe that together, these two mechanisms can enhance each other, and therefore, magnify the already powerful professional development practices occurring in many schools and districts across the nation.

For example, in some schools where teachers are engaged in action research, they engage in their research without the sustained, regular support of a PLC. We believe that when action research becomes a part of the work of a PLC, individuals' engagement in inquiry is more thoroughly developed and refined at each PLC meeting, deepening the learning and knowledge construction that occurs as well as the quality of the action research process. Furthermore, when action research becomes a part of the work of a PLC, there is a greater likelihood that the learning that occurs from individual teacher inquiries conducted into classroom practice will spill over into collective inquiries conducted by a group of teachers sharing a goal for school improvement.

Conversely, in some schools where teachers are members of PLCs without engaging in action research, the group's work targets supporting one another in reflecting deeply on practice. At each meeting of the PLC, rich conversation occurs about the topic of the day (e.g., a teacher's dilemma, looking closely at student work, fine-tuning a lesson plan to be taught the next day), but no specific target goal ties each meeting to the next. We believe that PLCs engaged in teacher research on their practice are enhanced as meetings are given a focus over time by developing individual or shared wondering(s) for exploration, looking at data, analyzing data, and making findings public.

In addition to unleashing the potential power of combining action research and PLCs, we know that the depth of learning that occurs through both teacher research and participation in PLCs is directly related to the facilitation and coaching that occurs. Cassandra Drennon and Ronald Cervero, researchers on adult learning, share:

> The day-to-day actions taken by the practitioner inquiry group facilitator profoundly influences a group and many of the results.... Facilitators, however, have attained only a subtle presence in the existing ... literature despite their central position. Little is known either about their strategies and tactics or the implications of their efforts. (2002, p. 194)

Hence, we wrote this book to help those interested in coaching or facilitating teacher professional growth as they combine two of the best practices professional development for teachers has to offer: teacher research and PLCs. When these two strategies are intertwined with one another, we believe the end result is a school characterized by teachers, students, and administrators who keep learning alive and improve schools. Roland Barth likens the critical nature of inquiry in schools to the potter:

> Just as potters cannot teach others to craft in clay without setting their own hands to work at the wheel, so teachers cannot fully teach others the excitement, the difficulty, the patience, and the satisfaction that accompany learning without themselves engaging in the messy, frustrating, and reworking "clay" of learning. Inquiry for teachers can take place both in and out of the view of students, but to teacher and student alike there must be continuous evidence that it is occurring. For when teachers observe, examine, question, and reflect on their ideas and develop new practices that lead toward their ideals, students are alive. (1990, p. 50)

Therefore, in this book, we share strategies and tactics for developing and coaching an inquiry-oriented PLC based on the work of hundreds of committed educators who have shared their learning experiences with us, as well as our own research and experiences facilitating teacher research and learning communities over the past twenty years.

WHAT'S IN A NAME?
THE IMPORTANCE OF CLARIFYING LANGUAGE

In Shakespeare's classic *Romeo and Juliet,* Romeo Montague and Juliet Capulet meet and fall in love. Yet, they are doomed from the start as members of two warring families. In the famous quote, "What's in a name? That which we call a rose by any other name would smell as sweet," Juliet tells Romeo that a name is an artificial and meaningless convention, and that she loves the person who is called "Montague," not the Montague name and not the Montague family. In essence, Juliet is sharing that what we name something is not as important as what that something is. We can also learn from Juliet's quote that it is always important to provide clarity for the names we assign to objects, as those names can hold different meanings to different people.

In education, whenever an innovation is introduced and gains popularity in the field, that innovation emerges and grows as it is interpreted by different teachers and researchers and applied to many different teaching contexts across the nation and the world. As such, like Juliet, it is not uncommon for educators to face problems of language. For example, the ways one district interprets and implements an innovation such as differentiated instruction may vary in both subtle and apparent ways from the ways a district across the country is implementing differentiated instruction. Both districts use the term *differentiated instruction* to describe their practice, but that term is not being used in exactly the same way by both parties.

Action research, professional learning communities, coaching, and *inquiry* are all terms that are currently being interpreted and applied in different, but related ways in classrooms and districts around the world. For this reason, before we move on, we believe it's important for us to clarify the ways we are using these terms in this book. We believe language is incredibly important, and we, ourselves, have struggled with which terminology will best paint a picture of the way powerful school-based professional development can play out in schools. We can't solve overarching language issues we experience in the field of education; innovations are constantly taking root and sprouting different variations and forms. But we can be clear about how we are using particular terminology in this text. Hence, in this section, we review definitions and offer clarification on the concepts and terms we used in the creation of our inquiry-oriented PLC model for school-based professional development.

Action Research

Over the past three decades, there has been a great resurgence of interest in action research (see, for example, Cochran-Smith & Lytle, 1999b). Action research actually has its roots in the work of John Dewey. Over the years, the term *action research* has been used interchangeably with other terms such as *classroom research, teacher research,* and *practitioner inquiry.* While these phrases have been used interchangeably, they do have somewhat different emphases and histories. Action research, for instance, usually refers to research that is intended to bring about change of some kind, usually with a social justice focus, whereas teacher research quite often has the goal only of examining a teacher's classroom practice in order to improve it, or to better understand what works. Exploring the emphases, histories, and different terminologies associated with teachers' systematic study of their own practice is beyond the scope of this text, but if you are interested in exploring the history and evolution of the teacher research movement, numerous texts are available, such as the classics *Inside/Outside: Teacher Research and Knowledge* by Marilyn Cochran-Smith and Susan Lytle (1993), or *Becoming Critical: Education, Knowledge, and Action Research* by Wilford Carr and Stephen Kemmis (1986). In this book, we use *action research* as an inclusive term to refer to the overarching process teachers and other educational practitioners (e.g., principals) use to seek out change and reflect on their practice by posing questions or wonderings, collecting data to gain insights into their wonderings, analyzing the data along with reading relevant literature, making changes in practice based on new understandings developed during inquiry, and sharing findings with others (Dana & Yendol-Silva, 2003).

PLCs

In the past decade, there has been a proliferation of discussions in both the education and business literature, as well as in schools across the nation, about "professional learning communities" and their ability to help institutions improve. For example, in *Professional Learning Communities at Work,* Dufour and Eaker (1998) argue, "The most promising strategy for sustained, substantive school improvement is developing the ability of school personnel to function as professional learning communities" (p. xi). The concept of PLCs took hold across the nation as many top scholars and leaders in education, including Linda Darling-Hammond and Milbrey McLaughlin (1995), Michael Fullan (2001), Peter Senge (1990), and Andy Hargreaves (1994), claimed that schools must become "learning organizations." However, according to Whitford and Wood (in press), there is a stunning lack of clarity about what actually is being proposed. "A wide variety of distinct professional development approaches, school social groupings, and change and improvement strategies appear in the literature labeled as 'professional learning communities'" (Whitford & Wood, in press, p. 2). For example, in the past decade, the terms *professional learning community, collegial study group,* and *critical friends group* have all been used interchangeably. Exploring the emphases and different iterations of the PLC is beyond the scope of this text, but we invite you to explore many of the excellent resources and writings about the PLC concept, such as Dufour and Eaker's (1998) *Professional Learning Communities at Work,* Roberts and Pruitt's (2003) *Schools as Professional Learning Communities,* Easton's (2004) *Powerful Designs for Professional Learning,* Whitford and Wood's (in press) *Teachers Learning in Community: Realities and Possibilities,* and the National School Reform Faculty's journal titled *Connections.* In this book, we define PLCs generically as small groups of faculty who meet regularly to study more-effective learning and teaching practices.

Coach

As previously explored in this chapter, traditional professional development for teachers (the "sit and get" model) occurs "separate from the classroom contexts and challenges in which teachers are expected to apply what they learned, and often without the necessary support to facilitate transfer of learning" (Killion & Harrison, 2006, p. 8). In the past decade, to address this weakness in professional development and to improve teacher and student learning, many school systems have carved out a new professional role for school-based coaches. According to Killion and Harrison (2006):

> School systems and states call it by many different names and describe its purposes and functions differently. Some of the titles for the position are coach, literacy specialist, math coach, instructional specialist, mentor, master teacher, or lead teacher. Whatever the name of this role, the job is complex. People in the job are part teacher, part leader, part change agent, part facilitator. (p. 8)

In this text, we define the term *coach,* to be inclusive of all of the roles Killion and Harrison name in the above quote, as "a teacher who has responsibility for, supports, and facilitates the professional learning of colleagues." All of the coaching roles described by Killion, no matter what the specifics of their coaching jobs entail, can implement and weave the inquiry-oriented PLC model described in this book into their coaching responsibilities and practice. When an educator weaves action research and PLCs together as a part of a coaching practice, we sometimes refer to that person in this text as *inquiry coach, PLC coach,* or *inquiry facilitator,* no matter what that person's official coaching role is called in the district. In some districts, where there is no designated full-time coaching role, department heads may receive one additional free-period in secondary schools to facilitate an inquiry-oriented learning community. Similarly, in elementary schools, grade-level teams might decide to function as an inquiry-oriented PLC, and the grade-level team leader might facilitate and coach the group.

Inquiry

Over the years, in our own coaching of action research, we became discouraged by the baggage that the *research* part of *action research* carried with it when the concept was first introduced to teachers. The images that the word *research* conjures up include a "controlled setting," "an experiment with control and treatment groups," "an objective scientist removed from the subjects of study so as not to contaminate findings," "long hours in the library," and "crunching numbers." Teachers, in general, weren't overly enthused by these images, and it took a good deal of time for us to deconstruct these images and help teachers see that those images were antithetical to what action research was all about.

So, over time, we began replacing the terms *action research* and *teacher research* with one simple word that carried much less baggage with it— *inquiry*. The term *inquiry* has also been used to refer to an instructional strategy in the teaching of science in which lessons are investigation-based. Of course, the term *inquiry* can also refer to the simple request for information a teacher makes to another teacher, the principal, or the district office. While *inquiry* has been used in different ways in the past, we refer to inquiry in this book as a disposition or stance that teachers take toward their practice. This disposition is characterized by an acceptance of the truth that teaching is an inherently complex endeavor. Because of the complexity teaching entails, it is natural and normal for many questions, problems, issues, dilemmas, and tensions to emerge throughout a teacher's career. The teacher commits to problematizing his or her practice to continually unearth and discover new questions about his or her own teaching. As questions emerge, teachers commit to intentionally and systematically studying these questions, learning from them in their own daily work. Engagement in an inquiry-oriented PLC is one way to actualize an inquiry stance toward teaching.

Inquiry-Oriented Professional Learning Community

In this book, we name a model for school-based professional development that combines some of the best of what we know about action research and PLCs, and in the process, addresses a weakness that has been defined in traditional professional development practices. We name this new entity the *inquiry-oriented professional learning community*. We define an inquiry-oriented PLC as a group of six to twelve professionals who meet on a regular basis to learn from practice through structured dialogue and engage in continuous cycles through the process of action research (articulating a wondering, collecting data to gain insights into the wondering, analyzing data, making improvements in practice based on what was learned, and sharing learning with others).

WHAT MIGHT AN
INQUIRY-ORIENTED PLC LOOK LIKE?

One might wonder what members of an inquiry-oriented PLC might do as they gather to explore their teaching practice and student learning. There are many configurations that the inquiry-oriented PLC might use, depending on the organizational structures and incentives that are available to support their work. School leaders need to understand that the degree of authenticity and acceptance of the PLC work will be highly influenced by the resources that they dedicate to creating time and space for the activity. In some cases resources only allow PLC groups to meet once a month to engage solely in each phase of the action research cycle. In other cases, PLC groups might be able to meet two or three times a month to engage in inquiry-oriented professional learning into a shared dilemma that is related to, but also moves beyond attending to the phases of the action research cycle. Whatever your situation, remember that starting small is better than not starting at all. Our only word of caution to the coach and school leadership is to be sure that you match your expectations for the work to the amount of time you realistically can dedicate to the work.

In an effort to illustrate what we mean by inquiry-oriented PLCs, we would like to provide an example of the ultimate model for this job-embedded form of professional learning. This example has four important features.

1. It engages teachers in an inquiry-oriented PLC meeting each week that is job-embedded and develops different types of teacher professional knowledge.

2. It is led by a school-based coach (in the following example, the math coach for the school) with both subject area knowledge related to the PLC work and knowledge of PLC processes.

3. Over time, the PLC meetings are characterized both by the use of protocols to structure dialogue as well as the action research cycle to gain insights into one shared and agreed-upon topic for inquiry.

4. The inquiry-oriented PLC work is viewed by the participants as a part of their professional responsibilities.

Example: An Inquiry-Oriented PLC
Explores Differentiated Math Instruction, Grades 4–5

Our ultimate example of an inquiry-oriented PLC takes place in an elementary school where Mr. Thomas, the math coach, meets a group of upper elementary teachers each Tuesday for one hour during a shared fourth and fifth grade planning period. Together, this PLC is exploring ways to differentiate mathematics instruction to meet the needs of all learners. This shared inquiry topic emerged during September as teachers in the upper grades of this school examined school data that indicated the bottom and top quartile students were not making the desired progress. Each teacher within the learning community has crafted a subquestion that connects to the overarching, shared question that focuses this PLC, "How do we differentiate mathematics instruction to meet the needs of all learners?" For example, Mr. Johnson, a fifth grade classroom teacher, and Mrs. Smith, the English as a second language teacher who spends the entire ninety-minute mathematics block in Mr. Johnson's classroom two days each week, have elected to study, "How does coteaching allow teachers to differentiate math instruction for their students?" Other teachers are inquiring into individual questions related to differentiation in math such as, "How does differentiating my assessment tools influence student learning?" and "How do I adjust mathematics curriculum content to meet the needs of struggling learners?" As a group, the entire PLC is committed to supporting each other's growth and student growth in the area of differentiation and mathematics.

As October began, Mr. Thomas, the math coach who was facilitating the inquiry-oriented PLC, identified a variety of tools that could deepen their inquiry work. During the first meeting of the month, Mr. Thomas realized that the teachers needed to deeply understand what differentiation meant and create an image of what differentiated instruction looked like in classrooms. Mr. Thomas realized that the internal knowledge did not exist at their school, so he identified one of Carol Tomlinson's books on differentiation and began a book study that helped teachers construct this new knowledge. Over the course of the year, Mr. Thomas continued the external knowledge thread by bringing in guests who were knowledgeable about differentiated instruction to speak with the group. By bringing in new knowledge from external sources, Mr. Thomas is acknowledging the importance of knowledge *for* practice but simultaneously realizing that he must make sure there are opportunities at other PLC meetings for teachers to move beyond the processing of disseminated information to engage in real and meaningful change in the classroom.

During the second meeting of the month, Mr. Thomas attends to the teachers' need to begin engaging in real and meaningful change in the classroom. To these ends, he creates an opportunity for teachers to really examine the kind of math work that the students were currently engaged in, as well as to get a sense of the learning that was and was not occurring. As a result, Mr. Thomas engaged the learning community in looking at student work that members brought from their own classrooms. By inquiring into their own student work, the PLC members deepened their local knowledge of their students, their curriculum, and their own planning.

As a follow-up during the third week of the month, Mr. Thomas asked teachers to bring dilemmas of practice associated with their early attempts at differentiation. Mr. Thomas used many protocols to facilitate these conversations and help the PLC members dialogue about ways to resolve these dilemmas of practice. During the second and third week, Mr. Thomas is purposefully identifying inquiry-oriented PLC activities that require teachers to test out new ideas that can create knowledge *in* practice and encourage dialogue about that activity that has the potential to generate knowledge *of* practice.

Finally, in the fourth week of the month, Mr. Thomas turned the group's gaze toward action research. Given that the group members had already identified their collective and individual wonderings, this fourth meeting in October focused on generating a plan for their inquiry and the development of a research brief, a short one- to two-page outline that contained the purpose of their action research, the stated wondering, how data would be collected and analyzed, and a tentative timeline for the project's completion. The knowledge development that Mr. Thomas had facilitated in the group during these earlier meetings jump-started the teachers' thinking about differentiating instruction in mathematics and provided early data for many of their research studies. By engaging in action research within the inquiry-oriented PLC, these educators had the opportunity to create all three types of professional knowledge construction: knowledge *for* practice, knowledge *in* practice, and knowledge *of* practice.

●　●　●

This illustration was offered to give the reader an image of what the inquiry-oriented PLC work looks like and why we believe inquiry-oriented PLCs are special forms of PLCs. In each of the activities—the book study, the student work examination, the dilemma investigation, and the action research—these educators shared a question that focused their collaborative work: "How do we differentiate mathematics instruction to meet the needs of all learners?" This theme gave content and meaning to all of the inquiry-oriented PLC activities over the course of the month, one activity of which focused on action research development. During the action research planning meeting, all teachers developed and received feedback on plans for their individual or shared research around questions that differed somewhat, but all related to the common theme of differentiated mathematics instruction (e.g., "How does coteaching allow teachers to differentiate math instruction for their students?" "How does differentiating my assessment tools influence student learning?" And, "How do I adjust mathematics curriculum content to meet the needs of struggling learners?"). Each member of the PLC was prepared to share, analyze, and inquire into the data with colleagues.

This example provides a glimpse of the ways action research and PLCs can commingle to create an inquiry-oriented PLC, and the ways this inquiry-oriented PLC work can play out in schools. In the remainder of this book, we continue to provide various examples and glimpses of the ways inquiry-oriented learning communities might look and tactics and tools for those who coach these important and powerful groups of teacher-learners. We begin the process by providing a detailed look at how to establish and maintain the health of an inquiry-oriented PLC in Chapter 2.

NOTE

1. Reprinted with permission from Roland Barth and Boston University *Journal of Education*.

2

Establishing and Maintaining a Healthy Inquiry-Oriented PLC

Creating a culture of inquiry rather than continuing to work in a culture of isolation represents a significant change within schools that must be supported. Systems successful in improving student learning are characterized by: articulated norms and values, a focus on student learning, reflective dialogue, collaborative practice, and deprivatization of teaching. (Garmston, 2007, p. 55)

Garmston summarizes the essence of the role a culture of inquiry plays in establishing a professional learning community (PLC) that will be powerful enough to promote student learning and school improvement. In Chapter 1, we highlighted the unique nature and culture of inquiry-oriented PLCs and suggested how PLCs and action research can merge to create powerful professional development. For PLCs to develop an inquiry-oriented culture, coaches must understand the roles, responsibilities, and activities that will promote this type of professional learning.

Coaching an inquiry-oriented PLC, characterized by a group of six to twelve professionals that collaborate on a regular basis to learn about their professional practice through structured dialogue and engage in continuous cycles through the process of action research (articulating a wondering, collecting data to gain insights into the wondering, analyzing data, making improvements in practice based on what was learned, and sharing learning with others), begins by the coach convening a group of interested individuals committed to creating a culture of inquiry rather than continuing to work in the culture of isolation described by Garmston in the opening quote to this chapter. Coaches cultivate this culture of inquiry within their PLC by continually assessing ten essential elements of a healthy PLC. The purpose of this chapter is to name and illustrate these essential elements so that, like a doctor, you can continually assess the health of your inquiry-oriented PLC, diagnosing areas that need attention and work to keep your PLC functioning and productive.

Before we explore our "Ten Essential Elements of Healthy Inquiry-Oriented PLCs," however, the overarching question you will need to ask is, "Is my group congenial or collegial?" This question is important to ask whether you are forming a new PLC or facilitating an existing one. There is a subtle, but important, difference between these two ideas. *Congeniality* refers to the friendly, cordial relationships some teachers have with one another in the work place. We see congeniality when teachers chat in the lunchroom about weekend plans, last night's football game, or the latest episode of *American Idol*. We might also engage in congeniality when attending birthday celebrations and retirement parties or sharing resources. According to Roland Barth (1990), congeniality is defined as "people enjoying each other's company" (p. 30).

Although schools need congeniality, congeniality does not alone promote teacher learning and professional knowledge construction. Congeniality alone will also not promote the development of inquiry-oriented PLCs. The dialogue that occurs in a purely congenial relationship excludes the kind of teacher talk that promotes wondering, thought, growth, and action. The type of relationship that allows conversation that promotes inquiry and professional knowledge construction is *collegiality*. Barth (2006) shares:

> Famous baseball manager Casey Stengel once muttered, "Getting good players is easy. Getting 'em to play together is the hard part." Schools are full of good players. Collegiality is about getting them to play together, about growing a professional learning community. (p. 11)

Collegiality moves beyond congeniality, and this movement takes work and risk on the part of both the coach and those being coached. Collegiality sets the stage for inquiry-driven PLC work.

Judith Warren Little (1981) offers coaches insight into four specific behaviors that characterize the conditions of collegial work. First, she emphasizes that adults in the school must have frequent, continuous, concrete, and precise *talk about their teaching practice.* Second, she emphasizes the importance of adults in schools *observing each other* engaged in the practice of teaching and administration and serving as critical friends to each other as they talk about those observations. Third, she describes the importance of teachers collaboratively *working on curriculum* by planning, designing, researching, and evaluating their curriculum work. Finally, Little discusses that adults in schools must become comfortable sharing their new craft knowledge by *teaching each other* what they have learned. Each of these activities is key to the work of inquiry-oriented PLCs and requires explicit attention by both the coach and the PLC members.

As a coach, you must realize that early PLC work requires establishing ways of being together that are often quite different than the typical cultural milieu of the school, as the opening quote to this chapter and our discussion of congeniality verses collegiality reminds us. You most likely will run up against challenges that will cause you to reflect, ponder, wonder if you should retreat, and eventually resolve and move forward. Establishing collegiality will rest on not only your ability but also the groups' ability to create a context that includes ten essential elements. The ten essential elements of healthy PLCs we describe in this chapter will help you determine the extent of collegiality that is present in your group, assess your existing learning culture, and intentionally select and introduce activities that can encourage a shift away from cultural norms that might inhibit collegiality and inquiry-driven PLC work. We illustrate each essential element through the work of Terry Campanella, an educator with many years of teaching experience, as well as a wealth of experience coaching PLCs and organizing PLC work in Broward County, Florida.

TEN ESSENTIAL ELEMENTS OF HEALTHY INQUIRY-ORIENTED PLCs

Essential Element #1

Healthy inquiry-oriented PLCs establish a vision that creates momentum for their work.

According to Thomas Sergiovanni (1994), "Community building must become the heart of any school improvement effort. . . . It requires us to think community, believe in community, and practice community" (p. 95).

From the beginning, your job as an inquiry-oriented PLC coach is to help the group establish and maintain a school improvement vision for the work that they are about to begin. How do you begin this effort when the group doesn't have a shared understanding of what the process of PLC work is in the first place? As a coach, you will need to help the members of your group create a vision that includes two components—*a vision for the process* that emphasizes how the community will use inquiry-oriented PLCs to work toward school improvement, and *an identification of the school improvement goals or dilemmas* that they will share. Both of these components are essential to establishing a collegial context for shared work to unfold.

Let's get a glimpse of Terry helping her PLC group create a vision for its work by first developing members' understanding of a PLC. Knowing that PLCs were new to the teachers she was working with, Terry began her first learning community meeting by helping members become familiar with how a PLC works. She selected an article titled "Building Professional Community in Schools" by Sharon Kruse, Karen Seashore Louis, and Anthony Bryk (1994) and used a text-based discussion protocol titled "Three Levels of Text" to help the group process the article.

The text-based discussion protocol was created by the NSRF, a group of educators committed to creating networks that support professional development focused on "developing collegial relationships, encouraging reflective practice, and rethinking leadership in restructuring schools—all in support of increased student achievement" (NSRF, 2007). Terry has found the Web site (http://www.harmonyschool.org/nsrf/default.html) and other NSRF resources invaluable to her work as an inquiry-oriented learning community coach.

Terry had become very skilled in selecting specific protocols to structure these text-based discussions and other PLC activities that used protocols throughout the year. She believes that when the right protocol is selected these protocols focus and deepen the reflection, dialogue, and processing that occurs within and between the group members. They help teachers within the learning community collaboratively construct the knowledge that is needed to begin working together.

Terry began the meeting, "I wanted to find an article that might provide us with an image of what an inquiry-oriented professional learning community might look like and I found this piece that looked like it could help us. It is called 'Building Professional Community in Schools.'"

Terry had wrestled with whether she should have the seven group members read the article ahead of time or if she should devote time during the meeting to read the article. She believed it would take about fifteen minutes for the group to read this article and decided that she would have them read the article at the meeting so everyone would be prepared.

Before they began reading, she also distributed the "Three Levels of Text" protocol to each teacher. She noted that the protocol would help them focus their reading and that part of the protocol asked the members to identify passages in the text as they read that they believed had important implications for defining the PLC's work. She then gave the group about fifteen minutes to read the article.

Once they finished reading, Terry reviewed the protocol instructions. The group would sit in a circle and engage in "rounds." A round consisted of group members taking turns sharing one of their highlighted excerpts from the article and reflecting on what that excerpt meant to them, followed by the group responding (for a total of up to two minutes) to what has been said. Sandra was the first volunteer. Sandra began her three minutes of reflection by reading the passage she had selected and sharing how she interpreted the passage, as well as how her interpretations connected and disconnected with her own past professional development activities. She then described the implications she believed the passage had for defining the PLC's work. After listening carefully, the group spent two minutes responding to her reflection. This process continued until all group members had shared using the same processing format. As the group was sharing, Terry charted the key ideas of the discussion on poster paper. This process continued until all seven group members had a chance to share.

Once everyone in the group had shared, the group took about five minutes to synthesize what they had learned, and then they debriefed the protocol process.

This activity allowed the group to create some key understandings about PLCs through focused dialogue. The debriefing process also allowed the group to critique the protocol process. By the time they had finished the text-based discussion, they had begun to chip away at answering the following questions: "What is an inquiry-oriented professional learning community?" "What are some of the structures, practices, and activities of inquiry-oriented learning communities?" And "Why should we create inquiry-oriented learning communities in our school?"

During each of the following meetings, Terry worked to deepen the group's answers to these questions. Terry realized that revisiting the PLC's goals and deepening members' understanding of the PLC work was critical if she was truly going to help them shift their work toward the inquiry-orientation she believed could lead to school improvement. A few weeks later Terry led the group in another protocol titled, "Chalk Talk." This protocol focused on all group members reflecting on their experiences and understanding of a committee, a PLC, and traditional professional development. As the protocol name, "Chalk Talk," alludes to, the "conversation" was not oral. The "chalk talk" was carried out in silence by each group member writing comments on a blackboard (in older schools), a whiteboard, or a big piece of chart paper hung on the wall. An example of the types of distinctions the group made between committee work and PLC work that were generated through Terry's "Chalk Talk" appear in Figure 2.1.

Figure 2.1   Distinguishing Between Committees and PLCs

Category	Committee	Learning Community
Purpose	Specific dilemma to be solved	Shared area of inquiry guides purpose
Duration	Ends when purpose is reached	Ongoing cycle of self-study
Focus	Concern for teacher participation in resolution	Concern for member changes in practice
Process	Decision-oriented	Reflection-oriented
Leadership	Designated leader/chairperson	Facilitator/shared responsibility
Tone	Formal	Informal
Use of Data	Focus on identified need	Focus on student data
Roles	Constant	Shifting
Structure	Traditional meeting structure/ hierarchical	Democratic meeting structure/ team-based
Goals	Specific goals from onset	Goals evolve from collaborative inquiry
Time	Bounded time period	Ongoing
Feeling	"Worker Bees"	Ownership
Individual/ Group	Consensus needed	Individual voice encouraged
Time	Meet as needed	Continuous

Terry realized how important it was for her PLC members to generate a clear distinction between the activities of PLCs and committee work. She knew from experience that creating this understanding is often what set successful groups apart from less successful groups. By engaging in the "Chalk Talk," they created a shared vision for collegial interaction and new ways of learning together within community.

Although developing a strong understanding of what an inquiry-oriented PLC does is essential, Terry's experiences coaching throughout the school year remind us that creating an understanding of PLCs is not enough to generate sustained commitment to teacher learning and school improvement. The second aspect of vision development requires creating a set of shared school improvement goals for the group's collective work. Terry has watched many PLCs focus on the development of the learning community roles, rituals, and responsibilities without delineating a clear, shared vision for how their work will connect to school improvement. Without a strong vision for school improvement, PLCs often lost steam over time and members started questioning, "What are we meeting about?" To avoid this, Terry dedicates time to creating a shared focus at another one of the early PLC meetings.

Terry began the meeting, "Today's goal is to generate a shared vision for our PLC work by identifying some areas of school improvement that can direct our work."

At the last meeting, the group had collectively identified resources that could help them with today's conversation. As a result, Terry had invited the principal, curriculum resource teacher (CRT), and the exceptional student education (ESE) teacher to the meeting to share student data that the group believed would be important to defining its work.

Terry asked each guest to share the data and emerging questions that he or she had about the school as the group looked at the data. As the group listened, the members noted the kinds of questions that were emerging and noted their own thoughts related to the data presented. Once each of the guests had shared, the group added their own insights to the list of wonderings based on their own classroom experiences. Terry took copious notes along the way, recording both the data and the group's emerging questions.

After hearing all the presenters and reviewing the data, Terry's group decided that the overarching question that would structure their PLC work would be, "How can we use differentiated instruction within our newly established inclusive classrooms to target and document the learning of our bottom quartile students?"

This question generated a great deal of interest and enthusiasm as it attended to the wonderings that emerged during the principal's, CRT's, and ESE teacher's presentations, as well as the felt difficulties or wonderings of the group members. The group had now identified a shared question that they felt passionate about collectively exploring during the school year. As a result, Terry facilitated a variety of activities that helped the members of her PLC explore this wondering. For example, members of the group engaged in a book study of differentiated instruction, used NSRF protocols to examine student work, and engaged in a variety of action research studies targeted at better understanding the needs of these bottom quartile students. By building the knowledge of what PLCs are and determining a shared focus for her PLC's work, Terry was able to cultivate a vision for PLC work, as well as create the momentum for focused inquiry around a shared goal for school improvement.

Essential Element #2

Healthy inquiry-oriented PLCs build trust among group members.

Educational scholars have long noted the critical importance of building trust among the adults within the school building and the correlation between trusting relationships and successful school improvement efforts. For example, Bryk and Schneider (2002) state:

Relational trust does not directly affect student learning. Rather, trust fosters a set of organizational conditions, some structural and others social-psychological, that make it more conducive for individuals to initiate and sustain the kinds of activities necessary to affect productivity improvements. (p. 116)

Michael Fullan (1999) also notes, "The quality of relationships is central to success [of school improvement efforts]. Success is only possible if organizational members develop trust and compassion for each other" (p. 37). As a result, building trust within the group becomes a critical component of a PLC coach's work.

The degree of trust the group members feel for each other will influence the depth of their collaborative inquiry work. It is important to note that the amount of trust individual group members have for each other and for you as their coach is directly related to your school's existing culture. Therefore, we cannot overemphasize the importance of understanding your school's existing culture as you ascertain how much PLC time you wish to spend on trust-building activities, and which type of trust-building activities would be most productive for your group. For example, if you are coaching in an underresourced school or an environment that is unforgiving, and/or working under high-stakes accountability pressures, the teachers in your group may feel less trusting and need more time to develop a sense of safety and build relationships. As a result, the coach will need to be sensitive to the amount of time the group needs to create congenial relationships and safety, and even to boost morale. In other schools, where morale is high and teachers are used to working collaboratively, PLCs will position themselves more quickly to begin the collegial inquiry work.

Terry offers some insights into how you can explicitly develop a more trusting and safe environment. One way that Terry sets the stage for trust to develop is by collaboratively establishing norms or ground rules for the group. She once again draws on the NSRF work by selecting a protocol to guide one of her group's early PLC meetings. The protocol is titled "Forming Ground Rules." Terry believes that norms are guidelines that establish parameters for the members' behavior. These guidelines can create a safe space for the group members to make themselves professionally vulnerable. In the following description of the group's "Forming Ground Rules" meeting, Terry leads the group in setting norms.

Terry began by explaining to her PLC the need for norms and how norms can support their collegial work together. To provide an example for the group, Terry shared that one example of a norm might be, "to start and end our meetings when we say we will." Next, Terry asked her group members to take a few minutes to respond to the question, "What conditions do I need to do my best learning in this group?"

After five minutes devoted to group members silently making an individual list, Terry asked each participant to name *one* thing from his or her list, going around in a circle, with no repeats. They were to complete as many circuits as necessary to exhaust all group rules individuals had put on their list. As group members shared responses, such as, "We need to respect each other," "Confidentiality is important," "We need to be willing to take risks," "It is important to respect discomfort and ambiguity as these feelings can lead to growth," and "We must not only allow but embrace mistakes," Terry listed all responses on chart paper, asking for clarification when needed. When the group was finished, Terry led the group in looking at the list as a whole, combining some items on the list and asking if everyone could abide by the final list of ground rules. She noted that if anyone disliked or didn't want to comply with one of them, they should discuss it and make a decision to keep it on the list with a notation of objection, remove it, or try it for a specified amount of time and check it again. All group members felt comfortable with the list of ground rules they had developed.

Terry saved the piece of chart paper stating the group's norms and brought that to each subsequent PLC meeting that was held throughout the duration of the school year. The chart paper was hung in the front of the room each time the PLC met.

These norms established by her group became a living document that would be revised as her group worked together. Terry made sure that the norms were reviewed at the beginning of each meeting and often drew on resources from the NSRF Web site for norm-setting protocols and advice.

Although Terry was committed to making public the group's norms for interacting with each other, she also was cognizant that whether a group became a safe place for collaboration would rest on the integrity, responsibility, and professionalism of each group member. As a coach, Terry made sure to keep a pulse on the level of integrity, responsibility, and professionalism that existed within her group and when she detected that work needed to be done to ensure the health of the PLC she would return the group to its norms.

Beyond establishing norms, Terry also led the PLC toward establishing deeper trust in their colleagues by making their concerns about the learning community process public. One excellent protocol for helping PLC members voice and discuss concerns is the NSRF's "Fears and Hopes Activity."

Following this protocol, Terry began a PLC meeting with, "What I would like you to do now is independently jot down two things—your greatest fear of participating in our PLC work this year as well as your greatest hope for participating in our PLC work this year."

After about five minutes, she asked group members to share their hopes and fears, and as they shared she generated a collective list of those hopes and fears on the chart for the group to review. Upon completing the list of group hopes and fears, Terry debriefed the activity by asking if members noticed anything surprising. She also asked them what they felt was the impact of expressing negative thoughts, as well as what policies and practices would be needed to reach their hoped-for outcomes.

By using this protocol and engaging in this dialogue, the group members identified how they wanted their group to be. As a coach, you will need to be open to all responses and seek input as to how the group might respond to these concerns. This type of checking in can be useful throughout the year as new hopes and fears are encountered.

Another exercise that Terry uses to promote trust-building is the "Community Agreements" protocol, also developed by NSRF. The community agreement establishes four principles that are critical to collegial study group work. These principles include show up and choose to be present, pay attention to heart and meaning, tell the truth without blame or judgment, and be open to the outcome but not attached to the outcome. These principles set the stage for both congeniality and collegiality. Terry introduces these community agreements as text to discuss by using a think/pair/share activity to help the group process these agreements.

She begins the process by first asking each participant to jot down one image of what each agreement would look like in action. Next, Terry pairs the participants and asks them to share their images with their partner. Finally, each pair reports out one image for each of the four agreements. At the end of the session, Terry would ask the group to discuss the degree to which these agreements connected to the work that they envisioned doing together. By integrating activities intended to build trust among PLC members and monitoring the pulse of trust within the group, Terry can move the group one step closer to engaging in inquiry-oriented PLC work.

Essential Element #3

Healthy inquiry-oriented PLCs pay attention to the ways power can influence group dynamics.

Defining, analyzing, and building power is a vital part of coaching in an inquiry-oriented PLC. Power is both dynamic and multidimensional. Power can get good work done or keep good work from getting done. Power is influenced by context, circumstance, and interest. As a coach, you will need to be cognizant of the way that power is used within your PLC to accomplish the vision your group has set.

One way to create a collegial professional learning environment is to make sure that the study group members understand the use and misuse of power. According to Hunter, Bailey, and Taylor (1995), five kinds of power exist. *Positional power* occurs when a person has a more powerful position than the other group members. For example, when a principal becomes a member of the PLC, members of the group might feel threatened due to the evaluative power a principal holds over his or her teachers. This does not necessarily mean that the principal should not join the group. However, group participants, the principal, and the coach need to be cognizant of the influence of a member with positional power. Within learning communities, positional power should not be used as the *tipping point* for decision making as the goal of the PLC is to develop shared understanding and equalize participant voices so that all members are heard and understood.

Assigned power occurs when the group assigns a person within the group a particular role. For example, as a coach, your position offers you assigned power and as a result you must constantly self-assess your own use of power. *Knowledge power* occurs when a group member has more specialized knowledge and experience in an area the group is exploring. For example, if the reading coach is a member of the group and the group has decided on a schoolwide reading focus, the reading coach would typically possess knowledge power within the group. Members who possess knowledge power are uniquely positioned to deepen the PLC's work. However, the coach, as well as the group members who possess that knowledge power, must self-monitor their participation, embrace members' questions, and include the concerns of others in the group.

Another influential form of power that can emerge within PLCs is *personal power.* Personal power results from the skills and qualities an individual possesses that makes others in the group look to this person as a leader. Recognizing and involving the teachers within the group who possess this type of power helps the coach jump-start the development of trust and deepen the group's work. There are always a few teachers who are the pioneers of innovation and more easily embrace the learning community work. By developing these members as cofacilitators and teacher-leaders you can begin distributing the PLC's facilitation across the group membership.

The most potentially divisive and unproductive form of power that sometimes emerges within a PLC is *factional power.* Factional power occurs when several people within the group act together to influence or dominate the group process. As indicated, power can be expressed in forms ranging from domination and resistance to collaboration and transformation.

Since the goal of PLC work is to bring all members along within an inquiry community rather than leave a portion of the group behind, your job as a coach is to help group members understand these sources of power. Throughout the year, Terry encouraged the individual group members to talk about power openly, and self-assess how the power structure influenced the group and how power could be more evenly shared within the group to enhance the group's effectiveness.

One of the exercises Terry led her group through focused on initiating reflection about power by focusing on personal assumptions and experiences. In this exercise, Terry encouraged the PLC participants to identify their own sources of power as well as challenges groups can face as a result of power.

Terry began, "This activity introduces the concept of power and helps us recognize our own power and potential." She handed out a copy of the different sources of power (Figure 2.2) and asked the group to read the handout. She asked them to think about their personal and professional experiences with these various types of power while reading and identify examples of each type of power with which they were personally familiar. She also asked them to note the positive (strengths) and negative (limitations) impact that different kinds of power could have on learning community work.

Once the group had completed the sources of power exercise, Terry continued the exploration of power by breaking the group up into triads and giving each group a large sheet of paper and markers. Working in groups of three, on one side of the paper they drew situations that made

Figure 2.2 Types of Power Handout

Types of Power	Strengths	Limitations
Positional power occurs when a person has a more powerful position than the other group members.		
Assigned power occurs when the group assigns a person within the study group a particular role.		
Knowledge power occurs when a group member has more specialized knowledge and experience in an area the group is exploring.		
Personal power results from the skills and qualities an individual possesses that makes others in the group look to this person as a leader.		
Factional power occurs when several people within the group act together to influence or dominate the group process.		

them feel powerful within the school and on the other side of the paper they drew situations that made them feel powerless.

Once each group had finished, they presented their posters to the rest of the group. Terry took notes about the themes that were emerging as the groups presented. After all the groups had presented, Terry pointed out the words the members used to describe experiences that illustrated discomfort with power. Group members responded with words such as *disrespect, putdowns, being ignored, denied opportunities,* and *isolation.* She then highlighted the words the members used to describe experiences where they felt empowerment. Group members often noted words such as *overcoming fear, being recognized by others, creatively solving a problem, caring for or helping others,* and *pushing myself to take action.* In an effort to summarize their collective wisdom about power, group members reflected on how the collegial PLC could help them feel more empowered to make school improvement, as well as what types of barriers they would need to avoid in order to engage in inquiry-oriented PLC work together.

Essential Element #4

Healthy inquiry-oriented PLCs understand and embrace collaboration.

Hunter, Bailey, and Taylor (1995) suggest that when it comes to collaboration "one + one + one + one = five" (p. 26). This unconventional mathematics is what happens when a group of teachers work together toward a common objective. When people work together they create synergy that helps move the group toward fulfilling the shared purpose. To date, teachers' work has been fairly autonomous, as classroom teachers have typically worked independently in their individual classrooms. Cushman (1999) describes the importance of collaboration to creating a culture of inquiry:

> Cultures of inquiry depend on adults and students collaborating in teams and networks, and they set up critically reflective processes and norms that guide them. These structures—grade-level or cross-grade teams, critical friends groups, school-university teams, leadership teams—include professional interactions among teachers, but also involve other people important to the work, inside or outside the school and community. To support this characteristic, the larger system, too, must replace its hierarchy with multiple networks of this sort.

A part of the coach's responsibility is to help create this mind-set toward more collaborative learning. By helping teachers see that working together yields greater results than working alone, the PLC can begin to create a culture of collaboration.

The goal of the inquiry-oriented PLC is to create a collaborative learning space within the school that focuses on teacher and student learning. Throughout the year, the coach must identify ways to inspire group members to work as a team, as well as encourage them to assume leadership roles within the group. As the group develops, the coach needs to include all group members in critically evaluating their progress toward effectively creating a collaborative learning space.

There are many ways to help groups reflect on the power of teamwork. The NSRF Web site offers many team-building activities for coaches to select from. One way that Terry helped her PLC members understand the importance of collaboration is by sharing the tale of the blind man and the elephant used by Lambert, Collay, Dietz, Kent, and Richert (1996) to highlight why collaboration leads to more learning than isolation. During a portion of the PLC meeting, Terry read aloud:

> Each of the men tries to describe the elephant by approaching it from a different perspective. One climbs a ladder, touches the elephant's trunk, and says, "An elephant is long, thin, and round like a rope." Another touches the elephant's side and says, "An elephant is hard, smooth, and flat like a wall." Still another touches the elephant's leg and says, "An elephant is round, firm, and tall like a tree." All of them are correct in their assumptions, and yet none of them understands the elephant. If they were to combine their descriptions, they might have a sense of the features of the elephant; yet they would still be lacking the gestalt, the wholeness of the elephant.

After sharing the tale with the group, Terry posed the following questions: (1) How does the tale metaphorically connect to PLCs?, (2) Why is inquiry more powerful when done within a community?, (3) How can we be sure not to function like the blind men within our own PLC?, and (4) How will collaboration make our work more powerful?

One form of collaboration that Terry has consistently noticed requires more support and encouragement is the movement to peer observation. Kruse et al. (1994) note that deprivatization of practice is key to collaboration. Based on Terry's experience, teachers who collaborate, share, observe, and discuss each other's teaching methods and philosophies demonstrate one of the deepest forms of collaboration. Terry has learned that peer observation requires the coach to help with both the logistics of arranging the observation as well as helping teachers feel comfortable taking the observation risk. Of course, logistical nightmares exist in finding time to observe a colleague in the classroom. However, resolving logistical barriers is probably the easier piece of the equation to solve. Teachers must feel comfortable sharing a practice if they are going to collectively inquire into that practice.

Preparing teachers for peer observation requires beginning the work within a relationship that they perceive as safe.

Helping teachers understand the importance of this type of collaboration as well as giving them tools that can help them feel comfortable exploring each other's practice is essential coaching work. Terry used the NSRF Web site to find protocols that provide structures that support peer observation targeted at learning from school and classroom visits. Some of these protocols include the "Collaborative Ghost Walk," "First Classroom Visits," "Pre-Conference Protocol," "Observing Students at Work," and "Peer Observation."

During one of the PLC meetings early in the year, Terry introduced eight different observation protocols to the group. She began, "At our last meeting we discussed the importance of peer observation to establishing collegiality within our group. Today I brought eight different protocols that can help us become more comfortable with observing each other and our context."

Terry asked the members to pair up and she gave each of the six pairs one of the eight protocols. She kept one for herself and saved the last protocol for another day.

Next, she asked each pair to take twelve minutes to read through the protocol and be prepared to share the purpose and process of the protocol with the other group members. She also asked them to identify the strengths as well as the barriers that might inhibit the use of this protocol using the graphic organizer found in Figure 2.3.

Figure 2.3   Graphic Organizer

Name of Protocol	When would I use this protocol? For what purpose?	Strengths	Weaknesses

SOURCE: Terry Campanella, adapted from the work of Debra Smith and Fern Tavalin.

After reading, discussing, and reflecting on the protocol, the pair shared its protocol with the larger group. Each of the PLC members had now become familiar with the protocols to support peer observation. Additionally, each PLC member understood how the protocols differed and how they needed to be purposefully selected for a particular use. Terry asked, "Which of these activities are any of you willing to try between now and the next meeting?"

After a brief discussion, one of the members agreed to pilot a protocol she believed would help her answer a specific question that she had about her bottom quartile students. She identified a colleague to work with and agreed to share with the group the results during the next PLC meeting. Terry also volunteered to pilot one of the protocols with one of the members in her PLC observing her teaching mathematics, an area that Terry believed she was not meeting the needs of her bottom quartile students.

As a coach, you can help other group members feel more comfortable with peer observation and collaboration by sharing these protocols at meetings, as well as modeling the use of these protocols within your own classroom. Peer observation is one of the ultimate acts of collaboration, as it requires teachers to make their actual teaching practice public to their colleagues and open to scrutiny. PLCs that regularly embrace collaboration such as peer observation are typically highly sophisticated groups who have developed trust in each other and an understanding of collective inquiry into a shared goal.

Essential Element #5

Healthy inquiry-oriented PLCs encourage, recognize, and appreciate diversity within the group.

Just like the lesson from the blind men and the elephant tale, individual members of a PLC come with diverse values, skills, knowledge, beliefs, philosophies, experiences, expertise, and perspectives. It is this type of diversity that generates energy for change, as well as the disequilibrium necessary for learning (Jacobs, 2007; Lambert et al., 1996). PLC coaches recognize that membership diversity is something to both celebrate and plan for.

Diversity is important to a PLC's work on multiple levels. First, PLCs function best when comprised of people with different perspectives, knowledge, skills, and dispositions. This diverse group membership is necessary for the group to prompt each member's thinking, question each other's assumptions, and engage in critical friendship. Without diversity, study groups can become entrenched in groupthink, which can become highly unproductive and may just perpetuate the status quo rather than move the group forward. Groupthink often results in hasty decisions, where individual doubts are set aside and ideas are not questioned. Coaches can help group members recognize the importance of diverse group membership to their learning, as well as the importance of allowing members both inside and outside of the group to disrupt the status quo. They acknowledge the importance of both insider and outsider knowledge:

> Cultures of inquiry are highly strategic and purposeful about seeking and using outside information, resources, expertise, and collaborations. Ideas, information, and people constantly move across their boundaries with the "outside." The larger system must provide access to information and support, networks for sharing and building knowledge, and non-hierarchical, ongoing partnerships, interactions, and critical friendships. (Cushman, 1999)

Coaches seek to make sure that diverse voices are heard within the group and that diverse perspectives are garnered from outside sources when the group lacks diverse knowledge and perspective.

In addition to acknowledging the importance of diverse knowledge bases to a PLC's learning, coaches can help members recognize the diverse ways that they approach learning. Effective PLC coaches, like Terry, not only consider the diverse ways participants approach learning, they also consider the diverse expertise of the group members and identify ways to best use the internal expertise. Good coaches identify critical junctures where bringing external expertise to the group will benefit teacher learning and the direction of the group's work. For example, the coach needs to systematically plan how the group will gain access to knowledge related to the school achieving the group's vision for improvement. This may mean that teachers read research-based articles from educational journals, observe teachers in other schools, visit a specialist, or listen to a guest speaker from the district who has strong knowledge in a particular area.

Each week, Terry works with the group members to identify when the professional knowledge found inside the group is not enough to maximize the group's learning and, when needed, Terry secures help from external sources. The goal of bringing in external knowledge is not to value external knowledge over internal knowledge but rather to provide opportunities for developing diverse perspective taking that allows the members to critically examine their own teaching practice. A healthy inquiry-oriented PLC is strengthened by the presence of a diverse set of perspectives brought to the group and inquired into through professional dialogue.

Essential Element #6

Healthy inquiry-oriented PLCs promote the development of critical friends.

According to the Society for Organizational Learning (Senge, 2007), developing capabilities for real conversation is not easy.

> Most of what passes for conversation in contemporary society is more like a Ping-Pong game than true talking and thinking together. Each individual tosses his or her view at the other. Each then responds. Often, we are preparing our response before we have even heard the other person's view. In effect, we are "taking our shot" before we have even received the other's ball. "Learningful" conversations require individuals capable of reflecting on their own thinking.

The challenge for coaches is figuring out how to make these kinds of "learningful" conversations happen within their PLC. Meaningful and practice-changing PLC work requires teachers to communicate with each other in ways that promote collegiality and result in teacher learning. The type of communication is referred to as *critical friendship*. The *critical* in *critical friends* means engaging in important, key, and necessary talk that carefully confronts and inquires into the issues being explored. This type of friendship is essential within an inquiry-oriented PLC. Trust is a prerequisite for this movement toward becoming critical friends. Once a foundation of trust is built, teachers can solicit and provide feedback that generates reflective thinking.

One way that Terry develops critical friends communication skills is by using a protocol developed by NSRF titled "Feedback Nightmares." Terry stated at a PLC meeting, "You have five to ten minutes to write about a bad experience you have had receiving feedback." Once the group had finished, Terry paired the participants to share their writing and generate a list of five dos and don'ts about giving and receiving feedback.

After completing the work in pairs, Terry asked the pairs to share with the larger group the list that they compiled and add any new ideas to the group's norms. Once they had all shared, Terry debriefed the activity by asking the group to discuss the value of this activity.

After exploring the group's experiences receiving feedback, Terry introduced the idea of "learningful communication" as providing each other with constructive warm and cool feedback when working together. She began, "Constructive feedback is a critical component of collaboration that moves people beyond congeniality to embrace collegiality. Warm feedback refers to supportive and appreciative statements about the work presented. Cool feedback refers to offering different ways to think about the work presented or raising questions."

Terry had found that if her group had not worked together frequently and the teachers in her school were not used to giving each other warm and cool feedback on their work, she needed to do feedback work with the group. Given that conversation is the heart of the PLC's work and the vehicle that drives changes in teacher practice, Terry attends to the nature of the conversation within the PLC as she cultivates critical friendship. She often incorporates two tools described on the NSRF Web site, "Feedback Principles" and "Feedback Carousel," to deepen each member's ability to engage in critical friendship. Feedback principles contain guidelines for giving feedback that include such statements as, "Give feedback with care," "Let the recipient invite it," "Be specific," and "Avoid evaluative judgments." Feedback principles also include guidelines for receiving feedback that include statements such as "Specify the behavior about which you want feedback," "Clarify your understanding of the feedback," and "Take time to sort out what you heard." By reviewing this document from time to time with her PLC group members, Terry keeps the notion of critical friendship fresh in their minds as they engage in PLC work together.

The "Feedback Carousel" involves all members of the PLC creating a display on a piece of chart paper depicting the significant elements of their plan for teaching an upcoming lesson, for action research, or for some other plan for work related to the PLC vision they will be doing in their classroom during the upcoming week. The coach encourages the use of color and creativity in the creation of the display. Next to each display, the coach hangs another piece of chart paper that is divided into four quadrants, each designated for a particular purpose—one for clarifying questions, one for probing questions, one for recommendations, and one for resources that might be helpful. The coach distributes a pack of small Post-it notes to every group member and asks them to rotate through as many plans as possible in an allotted time period, writing feedback on the Post-its and placing the feedback in the appropriate quadrant. The group then debriefs the entire process.

Terry believes this critical friendship will contribute to the degree to which the members inquire, as well as the sophistication of the learning achieved. She considers many feedback tools and activities such as the ones described above, in order to create the relationships that can move the conversations of her PLC group members from congenial to collegial, which allows the inquiry to deepen and the school improvement to occur.

Essential Element #7

Healthy inquiry-oriented PLCs hold the group accountable for and document learning.

As a PLC coach, one of your roles will be to document the group's collective work, support individual teachers in the documentation of their own work, and maintain the pulse of the health of the group itself. Documentation is essential as the data allows the members and coach to share their work with those outside of the PLC. By documenting success in terms of changes for students, you will be better positioned to acquire outside funds, compete for scarce internal resources, and perhaps even influence education policy. One of the best ways to document an inquiry-oriented PLC's work is through engaging in action research. This book describes in detail the way that coaches can help groups of teachers collaborate around the action research process. As will be demonstrated, the action research process requires the systematic and intentional documentation of teacher and student learning.

In addition to the action research process, another way Terry documents participation at PLC meetings is to ask the members to provide feedback at the end of a meeting using a reflection sheet. The sheet asks: (1) To what degree do you believe the PLC is improving teaching and learning? (2) To what degree did you feel involved in the day's session? (3) What will you take back to your classroom from today's session? And (4) What could have helped you learn better today? This data informs Terry's planning for the next group meeting and provides a trail of teacher learning from one session to the next. Another tool Terry uses for gaining quick feedback at the end of a study group session is the "Aha's" and "questions" response sheet (Figure 2.4). Group members jot down questions that arise for them based on the meeting, as well as "Aha" moments that occurred during the meeting. This sheet documents what new insights and new questions the group members are generating as a result of their work.

Given that ongoing assessment of the PLC's progress is essential, another tool Terry often uses to capture the group's progress is the "Vessel Activity." In this activity, the group or each individual within the group is asked to select a vessel that best represents the nature of the PLC progress being made. Some might pick a tugboat if they feel like they are dragging along, others might feel like they are on a cruise ship with all the resources they need close at hand, and still others may feel like they are paddling a kayak but that the journey is worth it.

Whatever vessel they metaphorically connect with at that time, they explain why they selected the vessel and place the vessel on a long piece of chart paper that represents a metaphorical river. Terry then asks the group to write on the river what barriers and facilitators exist that are influencing how the vessel is moving, as well as what participants have individually and collectively learned along the way. Sometimes this is done on sticky notes that are added to the river and boat. By having insight into the group's barriers and facilitators, you can make important decisions that can remove some of these inhibitors to inquiry. This activity provides your PLC the opportunity to reflect on its lived experiences and

Figure 2.4   Aha's and Questions Response Sheet

Figure 2.5 River Activity Example I

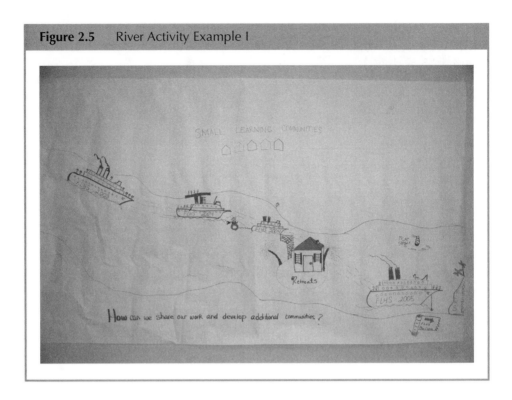

Figure 2.6 River Activity Example II

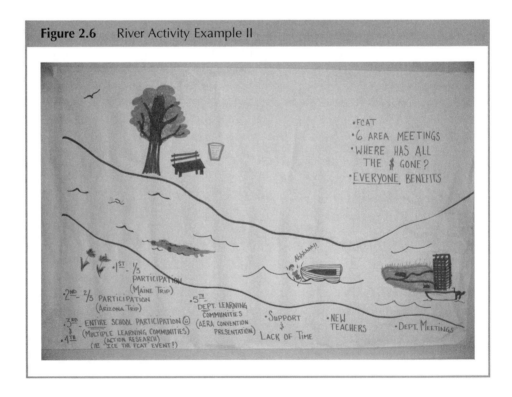

provide an honest picture of members' work as they progress through the year. Two rivers constructed by different PLCs Terry facilitated appear in Figures 2.5 and 2.6.

Essential Element #8

Healthy inquiry-oriented PLCs understand change and acknowledge the discomfort it may bring to some PLC members.

Coaches must be aware that change will cause some PLC members a great deal of discomfort. Change is full of uncertainty. "Change is a process of coming to grips with new personal meaning, and so it is a learning process" (Fullan & Miles, 1995, p. 408). One activity Terry has used to help her PLC members explore feelings about change is engaging in a book study using the book *Who Moved My Cheese?* by Spencer Johnson (1998).

Who Moved My Cheese? is a metaphorical story of four characters who live in a maze and look for cheese to nourish them and make them happy. Two of the characters are mice named Sniff and Scurry and two are "little-people" the size of mice, who look and act a lot like people. Their names are Hem and Haw. The reactions of these characters vary from quick adjustment to change to waiting for the situation to change by itself to suit their needs. This story is about adjusting attitudes toward change in life, especially at work. Change occurs whether or not a person is ready, but the author affirms that it can be positive. The overarching principles illustrated in the book are to anticipate change, let go of the old, and act as if you were not afraid.

Terry began her early learning community work by having her group read *Who Moved My Cheese?* before coming to the first PLC meeting. After reading the text, the group engaged in discussion around the following prompts:

- Describe the four characters' personalities or social styles.
- What does the cheese represent?
- What does the maze represent?
- What does the book say to you in relation to change?
- Which character do you resemble?
- What do you feel is the main message from the book?

Through the dialogue that transpired in response to the above prompts, Terry believed that group members became more self-aware as to how they respond to change and more sensitive of how their colleagues approach change.

Another activity that Terry uses to help PLCs she has coached explore their inclination to change is an adaptation of the NSRF's "Zones of Comfort, Risk, and Danger" protocol. In this activity, Terry instructed her group members:

> I'd like you to draw a diagram of concentric circles that looks like a target. Label the center circle "Comfort," the next circle "Risk," and the outer circle "Danger." The comfort circle represents the times when you feel most at ease, with no stress, and have a good grip on the topic. The risk circle represents the best opportunities for learning. It is where you are willing to take some risks, not know everything, and want to learn and take the risks necessary to do so. Finally, the danger circle represents times when you feel defensive or fearful. The danger zone is the least productive and desirable zone to work from. When you find yourself in the danger zone, it's best to work on some strategies to move yourself into the risk zone.
>
> Decide on what size you want to draw each of your circles depending on the quantity of time you usually work in that zone. Then, in each circle you are to note the various aspects or expectations of your work that make you feel really comfortable, that make you feel like there is some risk involved, and that get you worried and make you want to retreat. Write these work expectations in the comfort, risk, and danger zones respectively.

After PLC members complete their diagrams, Terry continues, "Once you have identified your comfort, risk, and danger zones, you will have greater insight into the areas in which you will experience more difficulty changing. By making this explicit, you will be better able to seek out support as you engage in that change." The activity ends with all individuals sharing what they learned about themselves through constructing their "Zone Maps."

A third activity that Terry uses is "Compass Points," also developed by NSRF. This is a protocol that Terry believes helps group members understand how each member approaches the change experiences differently. To lead this activity, Terry arrives to the PLC meeting early, and hangs four signs on each wall—North, South, East, and West. When PLC members arrive to the meeting, Terry explains the signs and the meaning they hold for understanding group work preferences:

> In this simulation, north represents the need to get moving on the change as quickly as possible. If you are inclined toward North, then just like the Nike commercial, your motto is "Just do it!" You love to act, try things, and plunge in. Now, South is quite different from North. If you are a "South" person, you need to have all

members of the group share their thoughts and be sure that everyone feels supported as they engage in the change. You are the caring direction, wanting to assure that everyone's feelings have been taken into account and that all voices have been heard before acting. Let's move over to the East now. East represents the need to understand the big idea or vision for the change. Before doing anything associated with a change, you want to understand the big picture and all the possibilities. Finally, West represents the need to have questions answered in detail. Before proceeding with any change, a "West" person likes to know the who, what, when, where, and why.

After reviewing each of the four directions, Terry asks each group member to reflect on the ways he or she typically responds to change, and physically move to the sign on the wall (North, South, East, or West) that best represents that person's response to change. Once all group members have placed themselves by a sign, Terry continues, "Now, within your group, I would like you to answer the following four questions and be prepared to report out to the larger group in about fifteen minutes. The questions are:

1. What are four strengths of your style?

2. What are four weaknesses of your style?

3. What is the style you have most difficulty working with?

4. What would you want others to know about your style?"

After each "Direction" group generates answers to the four questions, Terry asks each group to share its responses to the questions. As they speak, she has one of the group members chart the key ideas related to change that are expressed. Upon completing the protocol, Terry asks, "What did we learn about the diverse ways we can approach working and changing together?" The group notes that by engaging in this self-assessment and discussing the implications of the group members' different orientations to change, the group better understands and appreciates the diversity of its membership, as well as how members might be experiencing the change brought on by the PLC work.

Essential Element #9

Healthy inquiry-oriented PLCs have a comprehensive view of what constitutes data, and are willing to consider all forms and types of data throughout the PLC work.

Given the context of accountability in which educators work today, the goal that we seek as we work together in our PLCs is improved teaching with an eye on student learning. By inquiring together, we can discover ways to improve student learning and help one another improve teaching practices along the way. The coach can maintain this vision by insisting that student data is a regular artifact of the PLC group meetings. Data includes, but is not limited to, standardized test data, formative assessment, summative assessment, authentic assessment, performance-based assessment, student work, and attitude/surveys. By using multiple forms of data to drive our conversations and decisions, we keep the focus of our conversations on our students and their learning.

The type of data teachers bring to the PLC and examine as a part of their inquiry is important. As noted by Taylor (2002), teachers not only need to bring data but they need to bring all data—the good, the bad, and the ugly. A part of the PLC's culture must be the willingness to take risks and share the "ugly" data as well as the more successful examples of student learning. It is often effective for PLC coaches to share their own ugly data to model data selection for PLC members, as well as demonstrate their own vulnerabilities. For when all types of data are shared, PLC conversations will focus on student learning and teacher learning will occur.

Terry again uses the NSRF Web site to find and select numerous protocols that legitimize student work as data. For example, Terry uses the "Student Work Gallery" protocol adapted from the NSRF Web site as a tool for helping one group she worked with move from its PLC school improvement vision to improve writing instruction in their school to more specific questions about how to go about improving writing that each teacher can bring to the PLC conversations. Terry begins,

> In order for us to become more familiar with the kind of writing being done by our students, become aware of what we value about writing, and identify what we are concerned about, we are going to create a student work gallery during our next meeting. To do this, for our next meeting, everyone needs to bring at least one piece of your students' work in writing. In addition, I would like you to bring a question that the piece or pieces of student work you selected to bring to the meeting is creating for you.

As the next session began, Terry had PLC members hang the student work they brought to share and their accompanying question around the room. She then shared:

> Today I would like you to identify the progressions, holes in the progression, spiraling, repetition, and differences in approaches that will help us become familiar with the "whole" of the students' writing experiences in our school. To do this, we will do a walk

through the student gallery. Your goal is to notice the questions being posed about the work and respond to those questions using nonjudgmental statements by focusing on what the student is trying to do and what the teacher believes or wants for her students.

At this point, Terry asked the group to take the next thirty minutes to walk around the room and look in detail at the student work shared. During this time, Terry asked the group members to write their thoughts on Post-it Notes and stick them to the student work. She suggested that they might share questions they have about the work or what questions that they might have for the student.

Finally, Terry asked each group member to engage in a personal piece of reflective writing that focuses on the question, "What does looking at this work by these students make me think about my writing practice?" The gallery walk ends when these reflections are shared with the larger group. As a result of looking at this student data (writing samples from across the school), this PLC could identify strengths and weaknesses of the school's writing program.

This is just one example of how a PLC can use data to drive inquiry-oriented PLC discussions. As a coach, it is important to remember that the data that is useful to teachers comes in many forms. At times, useful data may be quantitative and in the form of test scores. However, useful data can also take the form of student work, teaching artifacts, and teacher dilemmas. The NSRF Web site has many protocols that facilitate discussion around different types of data. Data is an essential component of a healthy PLC as the data allows educators to identify important problems of practice that are deserving of their attention.

Essential Element #10

Healthy inquiry-oriented PLCs work with building administrators.

According to DuFour (1999), principals have been called on to: (1) celebrate the success of their schools and to perpetuate discontent with the status quo; (2) convey urgency regarding the need for school improvement and to demonstrate the patience that sustains improvement efforts over the long haul; (3) encourage individual autonomy and to insist on adherence to the school's mission, vision, values, and goals; and (4) build widespread support for change and to push forward with improvement despite resisters, and approach improvement incrementally and to promote the aggressive, comprehensive shakeup necessary to escape the bonds of traditional school cultures. For these reasons, principal support is critical to inquiry-oriented PLC work and inquiry-oriented PLC work is critical to the effective leadership of the principal.

For principals to truly understand and support the inquiry-oriented PLC work, the principals must possess a lived understanding of the nature and purpose of the work. PLC participation by principals develops their understanding of PLC work beyond what they can read in a text and also familiarizes themselves with faculty concerns about student learning needs within the school. This enables the principal to become a more informed instructional leader.

Although each of the previously mentioned essential elements of a healthy PLC is critical for successful PLC work, Terry has found that without a strong working relationship and support from the principal, PLC groups will not reach their potential. Those engaged in facilitating a PLC must recognize the importance of the school administrator and plan for his or her involvement. The principal must not only understand the process of PLC work, but must question, investigate, and seek school improvement solutions alongside the teachers. Whether or not the principal is a member of your PLC, the school administrator needs to provide the organizational and structural supports for this collaborative work to take place. For example, coaches engaged in PLC work sometimes encounter negative participants or those who refuse to do "extra duty" without extra pay. By working closely with the principal and other district administrators, coaches can identify organizational incentives that can support and integrate inquiry-oriented PLC work into the existing structures. For example, some districts have been able to integrate participation in an inquiry-oriented PLC into the teacher's professional development plan (see, for example, Chapter 6) and other districts have allowed teachers to use the PLC work toward the teacher's recertification credits. In addition to these creative incentives, some districts have recognized the value of utilizing their National Board Teachers as coaches for inquiry-oriented PLCs.

In addition to identifying incentives to participate, some principals who believe in the power of inquiry-oriented PLCs dedicate time to the work as well. For example, some principals we have worked with identified and scheduled a planning period each week to make it possible for grade-level teams (in elementary schools and middle schools) and departments (in high schools) to engage in PLC work focused on a shared goal during the school day. Others have used weekly early release days or dedicated weekly team meetings or monthly faculty meetings to this form of professional learning. Still others have used innovative scheduling options to free up teachers across their buildings to collaborate during the day, and a few principals have begun infusing online tools for PLC work.

When coaches, like Terry, take time to collaborate with district and building level administrators, they can identify organizational structures that can naturally support the work, making it "a part of" rather than "apart from" what is expected of teachers in today's classroom. Teacher professional learning is a part of what good teachers should be engaged in as a part of their daily work. When school administrators are on board, they can help with dedicating time, establishing communication procedures, finding meeting sites, accessing data, and providing resources that can support the work.

Although structural and organizational supports are important, the principal must be the "keeper" of the school's vision and demonstrate visible commitment to teacher learning through inquiry-oriented PLCs. A part of Terry's work is to help the principal she works with realize that when teachers perceive that authority and power are invested exclusively in the hierarchy of administration and that shared leadership isn't a goal, there is little interest in collaboration. When there is little interest in collaboration, teachers will retreat to the classrooms and close their doors. By keeping the focus on this shared purpose, continuous improvement is possible. Terry's work helps facilitate the vision as she works *with* the principal to enhance relationships "between the principal and teachers, among the teachers, and between the teachers and the students that enable risk taking, coaching, and giving and receiving feedback, and reflection to guide improvement" (Taylor, 2002, p. 43).

One way Terry helps the principal maintain a connection with the group is by frequently communicating the successes and progress that the PLC is making. By keeping these lines of communication open, the principal can help a coach acknowledge the important work that is going on within the PLC. We know that what gets rewarded and acknowledged is what gets done. By acknowledging the group's efforts, the PLC work is not something that is just taken for granted by the administrator, and the administrator seeks ways to make PLCs a part of the daily work of teachers, rather than an add-on to their already full days.

In addition to these reasons to collaborate with the principal, coaches also need to be able to secure the necessary resources to support the group's inquiry process. They may need resources for development, implementation, and/or data analysis. If the principal understands the power of healthy PLCs, the coach has communicated the focus of the inquiry to the principal along the way, and the work ties to student learning, securing necessary resources for PLC work is much more likely to happen.

ASSESSING THE HEALTH OF YOUR PLC

The job of a doctor is twofold. First, doctors provide well-patient care by seeing patients for regular check-ups and assessing that all systems in the body are functioning properly and working together to ensure the overall health of the patient. Second, doctors see patients when they are ill, diagnose the problem, and prescribe a course of treatment to bring the patient back to good health again.

Similar to the doctor, your job as a coach of an inquiry-oriented PLC is to use the ten essential elements we discuss in this chapter to regularly reflect on the PLC you are coaching to be sure "all systems are healthy." To review, these "systems" include: establishing and maintaining a vision, building trust, understanding power, enhancing collaboration, appreciating diversity, becoming critical friends, documenting learning and keeping group accountable for shared goal, gaining comfort with change, using multiple forms and types of data, and working with the school leadership. These systems are not mutually exclusive but build on and influence each other. Figure 2.7 provides a summary of the essential elements of a healthy PLC that were explored in this chapter, and it can be used as a handy guide to regularly assess how your PLC in functioning and make decisions about areas that need more attention.

Like Terry, you can select activities and protocols to guide discussion that help your PLC grow in the area diagnosed as needing more attention. For, according to DuFour (2004):

> The professional learning community model has now reached a critical juncture, one well known to those who have witnessed the fate of other well-intentioned school reform efforts. In this all-too-familiar cycle, initial enthusiasm gives way to confusion about the fundamental concepts driving the initiative, followed by inevitable implementation problems, the conclusion that the reform has failed to bring about the desired results, abandonment of the reform, and

Figure 2.7   Essential Elements of a Healthy PLC

Top Ten List: Essential Elements of a Healthy PLC

Healthy PLCs . . .

1. Establish and maintain a vision for their work.
2. Build trust among group members.
3. Pay attention to the ways power can influence group dynamics.
4. Understand and embrace collaboration.
5. Encourage, recognize, and appreciate diversity within the group.
6. Promote the development of critical friends.
7. Hold the group accountable for and document their learning.
8. Understand change and acknowledge the discomfort it may bring to some PLC members.
9. Have a comprehensive view of what constitutes data, and are willing to consider all forms and types of data throughout their PLC work.
10. Work with their building administrators.

the launch of a new search for the next promising initiative. Another reform movement has come and gone, reinforcing the conventional education wisdom that promises, "This too shall pass." (p. 6)

The success of your PLC depends not on the merits of the "concept but on the most important element in the improvement of the school—the commitment and persistence of the educators within the group" (DuFour, 2004) and the coach who leads them. Your role as an inquiry-oriented PLC coach can make or break the authenticity and impact of the work you facilitate.

For this reason, we recommend you visit the NSRF Web site (http://www.harmonyschool.org/nsrf/default.html) for clear instructions on each of the protocols that Terry used with her PLCs, as well as a large selection of additional protocols and activities you can use to keep your PLC healthy and moving forward in its important work! In addition, if you have not already participated in NSRF training, we encourage you to learn more about the foundation of PLC work and strategies for coaches by attending one of NSRF's Critical Friends Training Sessions.

We must also note that in this chapter, we list the top ten essential elements of healthy PLCs. These essential elements are *our* top ten picks based on our own coaching work and focus on the "dos" of coaching PLC work. However, these top ten essential elements of healthy PLCs do not exhaust all of the many factors that contribute to an effective and highly functioning PLC. For example, the NSRF also shares a list of five things *not* to do as a new coach. This list includes: (1) Don't set yourself up as the expert, (2) don't facilitate every protocol session yourself, (3) don't spend any whole meeting on team building, (4) don't stay in everyone's comfort zone, and (5) don't allow your group to become alienated from the rest of the faculty. While not exhaustive, our "Essential Elements of a Healthy PLC" list is certainly enough to get you started in the process of continually reflecting on the state of your PLC, and ascertaining the next best steps in moving the work of your PLC forward.

USING ACTION RESEARCH TO ADVANCE INQUIRY-ORIENTED PLC WORK

One way to move your inquiry-oriented PLC forward, deepen your documentation, and help connect the learning to the classroom is through weaving the process of action research into the regular meetings and agreed-upon work that your PLC has decided to engage in. To review, action research is defined as systematic, intentional study by teachers of their own classroom practice (Cochran-Smith & Lytle, 1993). Action researchers seek out change and reflect on their practice by posing questions or "wonderings," collecting data to gain insights into their wonderings, analyzing the data along with reading relevant literature, making changes in practice based on new understandings developed during inquiry, and sharing findings with others (Dana & Yendol-Silva, 2003).

By carefully studying our own and other PLC coaches' facilitation of action research, we have learned that there are four critical junctures in the action research process that strengthen the inquiry process. Critical junctures are places in the inquiry process where decisions that are made during this phase of the process greatly enhance or inhibit the depth of learning that can occur throughout the course of the inquiry. Critical junctures are also places that often cause teachers some discomfort or uncertainty. These junctures include: (1) locating an action research question or wondering, (2) developing a plan for research, (3) analyzing data, and (4) sharing work with others.

To help you develop a vision for how the process of action research can be intricately intertwined with the work of a new or established PLC, in the next four chapters we explore each of these critical junctures in depth, sharing stories of PLC coaches as they facilitate group members' development of questions or wonderings for study, develop an action research plan, analyze their data, and share their work with others.

3

Helping PLC Members Locate a Wondering

- *How do I maximize the use of a science notebook as a tool for learning and organization for ninth grade integrated science students?*
- *What is the relationship between students' journaling and their development as writers in Spanish class?*
- *What are parent and student perceptions of online grade books?*
- *How do I balance the provision for extensive responsive feedback on student writing in English class with the class time and teacher time it takes to provide such feedback?*
- *How does our school address the high-mobility rate of the migrant worker population we serve?*
- *How do we create more inclusive educational settings in our school?*
- *How do we improve the reading scores of our bottom quartile students?*
- *In this era of high-stakes testing and accountability, how do we enrich the curriculum for gifted students?*

Igniting the process of action research within a professional learning community begins by PLC members articulating a burning question they have about their practice. Burning questions, often referred to as *wonderings*, emerge from issues, tensions, problems, and/or dilemmas teachers face when confronted each day with the complexities inherent in the daily act of teaching. PLC membership wonderings can be individual or collective. Individual wonderings occur when members of a PLC decide to look deeply into their own classroom practice. Each member of a PLC then formulates his or her own question, and PLC members support each other by offering advice, suggestions, and critical comments about each PLC member's inquiry as it unfolds. The first four questions that open this chapter are examples of wonderings explored by individuals in a high school PLC.

Alternatively, collective wonderings occur when all members of a PLC elect to explore a single wondering or a series of related wonderings together. The collective wondering(s) may emerge from a common-felt difficulty across teachers and grade levels, or in response to whole-school data sets, such as standardized test scores. Members of the PLC work together to plan the inquiry, divide the plan into discrete components, and then divvy up each component to members of the group to complete in-between PLC meetings. The final four questions that open this chapter are examples of wonderings explored together by PLCs at four different school sites. Figure 3.1 provides some additional examples of wonderings explored by teachers in different grade levels and teaching areas to illustrate the scope and variety possible in wondering development. The few examples of questions by grade level and teaching areas listed in this chart are by no means exhaustive of the many possibilities for types of wonderings that might be explored, but they can serve to jump-start the wondering brainstorming process for the teachers you coach.

Whether your PLC members decide to explore individual or collective wonderings, or a combination of the two, it is important to note that:

> Rarely does any teacher researcher eloquently state his or her wondering immediately. It takes time, brainstorming, and actually "playing" with the question. . . . By playing with the wording of a wondering, teachers often fine-tune and discover more detail about the subject they are really passionate about understanding. (Dana & Yendol-Silva, 2003, p. 47)

Hence, one critical component of coaching inquiry within your PLC is creating a space for teachers to play. The purpose of this chapter is to help you create a playground for wondering development.

THE WONDERING PLAYGROUND

Qualitative researchers Robert Sherman and Rodman Webb (1997) argue that powerful research questions emerge from "felt difficulties." Teachers are constantly faced with felt difficulties or dilemmas as they reflect in and

Figure 3.1 50 Examples of Wonderings by Grade Level and Teaching Area

Elementary (K–5):	
Math	• How does one teach fractions conceptually, and what are the impacts of that teaching on the different learners in my classroom? • What is the relationship between students' basic math fact fluency and their ability to problem solve? • How can I differentiate instruction and use our district's adopted math program?
Language Arts	• How can I use my word wall in a literacy center to make it more meaningful for my students? • What is the relationship between the reading of fractured fairy-tale plays and the fluency development of fourth graders?
Science	• How can I encourage students to use scientific terms when talking about science? • How do online demonstrations compare to live demonstrations regarding effectiveness in capturing students' interest? • How can I take a science unit that is heavy on content and make it more inquiry-based?
Social Studies	• How can the story of the "true discovery" of America be taught to fourth graders in a developmentally appropriate way? • How will the implementation of the organizational structure embedded in interactive notebooks help our students understand the scientific process and gain historical perspectives in social studies? • How will using role play and simulations increase student understanding of historical events? • How do I begin to engage students in discussing difficult and controversial issues?
Secondary (6–12):	
Math	• How does the use of tessellations as a context for students to investigate geometric shapes and their properties play out in my classroom? • How can I instill in my seventh graders a habit of working through math problems on multiple choice tests so they do well on our state standardized test?
Language Arts	• What happens when I put culturally relevant literature in the hands of my eighth grade reluctant readers? • How will the use of comprehension strategies affect student reading achievement in the area of vocabulary? • What are some strategies I could use to facilitate better literature discussions?

(Continued)

(Continued)

Science	• How can I better utilize demonstrations in a way that empowers my students' learning of high school chemistry? • What is the relationship between investigations I typically use and my students' developing understandings of Bernoulli's Principle?
Social Studies	• How does using technology such as Google Earth impact students' understanding and application of geography skills? • How will deepening my own adult content knowledge and understandings about the Holocaust translate into the ways I teach this topic?
Special Areas:	
Art	• How can still life drawing help children see multiple perspectives, and apply this to social situations? • What is the relationship between students' expressing themselves through art and their writing for language arts assignments?
Music	• Which music and movement techniques can help improve my students' behavior during large group/circle time? • How can I teach music theory in a performance-oriented class? • How might music help a particular student combat some frustrations when reading and boost her self-esteem?
Foreign Language	• In what ways can I improve my students' ability to write in French? • How does keeping a daily, personal journal help Spanish students improve written grammar?
Physical Education	• What are the best ways to grade students in physical education class? • In what ways can physical education activities build on students' learning to read in kindergarten and first grades?
Technology Education	• How can a team of teachers work through problems together and support each other to overcome hurdles when using new technologies? • How can the use of assistive technologies (AlphaSmart, Kidspiration, audio recordings, and Stationary Studio) increase the writing quality, interest, and motivation for a gifted third grade student? • How can I use a SMART board to best facilitate student learning?
Administration:	• What are teachers' level of satisfaction with the current block schedule in place at the secondary level? • What are viable alternatives to ISS (in-school suspension) and how do they play out in our high school? • What are some strategies for promoting teacher leadership in my school, and how are they working? • In what ways does peer-coaching contribute to the continued professional development of veteran teachers and what role can I play as a principal to facilitate the process?

| Generic Act of Teaching (K–12): | • How can I better communicate with my middle school students' parents?
• What are the most effective methods to ensure that show and tell is a meaningful, academic-related activity?
• How do I design an extension of the reciprocal teaching method that is both effective and efficient, while still engaging to students?
• How can I incorporate more higher-level questions into classroom discussions, and have students recognize and answer them as such?
• How can we make inclusion meetings more helpful for students and educators in our school?
• What impact will a Critical Friends Group have on the teaching and professional growth of members of the group?
• How can students be taught organizational skills and strategies so they will use them to improve their academic performance?
• How do the structure and management of my classroom affect a particular student's behavior?
• How does my questioning behavior change as I teach across subjects?
• How can I use my students' social skills to enhance their learning and instruction at the same time?
• How do the ways I phrase questions contribute to how learners interpret them?
• In what ways do my classroom management and practices deter from my philosophy of teaching and my beliefs about how children learn?
• How can I maintain an inclusive classroom when high-stakes testing seems to encourage noninclusive practices? |

on their acts of teaching. As a result, these felt difficulties are direct concerns that emerge from one's own teaching experiences.

Establishing your playground begins by creating a space for members of your PLC to discover, share, and reflect on their felt difficulties or real-world dilemmas. It is in this space that healthy, meaningful wonderings are born.

Coaches can use a variety of tools to create this reflective space. For example, in our coaching work, we have asked teachers to progress through a series of exercises in relationship to eight teaching passions—"Helping an Individual Child," "Enriching Curriculum," "Developing Content Knowledge," "Experimenting with Teaching Strategies and Techniques," "Exploring the Relationship Between Beliefs and Classroom Practice," "Exploring the Relationship Between Personal and Professional Teaching Identities," and "Advocating for Social Justice." These eight passions, constructed based on our research and analysis of more than 100 teacher inquiries, are areas ripe for the development of wonderings (Dana, Yendol-Hoppey, & Snow-Gerono, 2006; Dana & Yendol-Silva, 2003).

To exemplify, one exercise related to the passion, "Helping an Individual Child" involves creating a three-column chart naming each student in a teacher's class, something unique or notable about the student, and a question that if answered, would give the teacher insights into that student's uniqueness. When completing this exercise, Jenn, a first grade teacher, paused at the fourth student's name listed on her chart—Meg. It was easy to fill out the next column, something unique or notable about the student, as Meg was often observed singing throughout the day and had a most incredible voice. Jenn wrote the word *musical*. In the next column, a question about the student, Jenn reflected on Meg's difficulty learning to read and her poor auditory processing skills diagnosed through testing. Jenn wrote, "How can Meg be so musical, memorizing music and lyrics to songs easily, and be having difficulty with reading?" After Jenn completed this same process for the remaining members of her class, she gazed at the entire list, and her eyes kept returning to the fourth row on her table—Meg, a student who had puzzled her for some time. Why had she never explored putting Meg's apparent musical gift to work on her reading? Completing this exercise led Jenn to design an action research study that did just that. Jenn's inquiry questions were, "In what ways could I use music to help Meg become a better reader?" and "How might music help her combat frustrations when reading and boost her self-esteem?" Additional exercises for exploring each of the eight passions can be found in one of our earlier books, *The Reflective Educator's Guide to Classroom Research: Learning to Teach and Teaching to Learn through Practitioner Inquiry* (Dana & Yendol-Silva, 2003).

Protocols are another tool coaches can use to help members of their PLC explore tensions in practice that may yield inquiry wonderings. In fact, Linda Emm and Pete Bermudez, NSRF coaches in Miami Dade school district in Florida, adopted the passions from our text to create a protocol for exploration with teachers in their PLC trainings (Emm, 2007). In this protocol, teachers read paragraph profiles of each of the eight passions, and select the passion that most accurately describes who they are as an educator. Next, teachers identify others in the room that have identified the same passion, and discuss what it is like to have this passion. After that, each person in the group privately identifies an actual student, by name, who has been affected by the group's profile and writes responses to the following questions:

- What have I done with this student?
- What's worked? What hasn't?
- What else could I do?
- What questions does this raise for me?

After this silent individual writing time, group members discuss the questions that teachers who share this passion are likely to have about their practice. A recorder lists these questions on newsprint, with the passion profile number at the top of the newsprint page.

After briefly hearing reports by each group and viewing the questions generated by each group on newsprint, Pete and Linda lead a discussion based on the following questions:

- What strikes you as you listen to the passions of these educators?
- Which of the questions generated intrigues you the most? Why?
- How might you go about exploring this question with colleagues?
- What would you do first?

You can adapt the protocol Pete and Linda developed and use it at one of your PLC meetings to help stimulate thinking about potential wonderings, or to introduce the notion of teacher inquiry to members of your group. Specific directions for the use of the protocol and the passion profile descriptions can be found at the end of this chapter.

A third way coaches can help group members explore the space where wonderings are born is through looking closely at PLC work documentation tools utilized over time. One documentation tool we have observed numerous coaches use is called the I-MAP, which stands for Individual Monthly Action Plan. Members of a PLC complete a monthly action plan individually or collectively at the close of a PLC meeting. The purpose of the I-MAP is to translate the learning that has occurred during a PLC meeting into teachers' practice and to provide continuity from one meeting to the next. Each individual or the entire group states a planned change they will make in practice based on what they learned from the PLC work during that meeting. Then, four columns are completed as teachers answer the questions: (1) Why am I planning to do this? (2) How will I initiate this change? (3) What supports do I need to be successful? And (4) How will I know if I've made progress? Figure 3.2 illustrates the I-MAP form. Looking at the I-MAPs the group completed over time can lead toward some powerful discussions about wonderings.

Once a coach has created space for group members to explore dilemmas or tensions in practice, the next step is to dedicate one or more of your PLC meetings explicitly to wondering development. If PLC membership decides to investigate individual wonderings, each member of the PLC comes to the wondering development meeting ready to share question(s) he or she is considering for exploration through inquiry. Sometimes coaches ask individuals to journal prior to coming to this meeting, or to complete a reflective guide. Figures 3.3 and 3.4 share examples of a journaling prompt and a reflective guide developed by Terry Campanella, the PLC coach featured in Chapter 2, to prepare her PLC members for their wondering meeting. At the wondering meeting itself, each individual takes a turn sharing the felt difficulty, dilemma, or tension in practice that has led to the question, and subsequently articulates his or her initial question. Dialogue about the dilemma and question helps each individual refine and further develop his or her wondering.

Figure 3.2 Individual Monthly Action Plan (I-MAP) Form

Individual Monthly Action Plan (I-MAP)

What implications does our collaborative work have for your practice between this meeting and the next? What change will you make in your work with students, their families, or your colleagues?

Planned Change: (What will I do?)

_____

_____

Why am I planning to do this?	How will I initiate this change?	What supports do I need to be successful?	How will I know if I've made progress?
What do I hope will happen as a result of this change in my practice?	What am I going to do? What steps will I take and when will I take them?	Who can help me and what do I need from them?	What evidence will I review? How will I document my growth?

SOURCE: http://www.harmonyschool.org/nsrf/protocol/doc/imap.pdf

Figure 3.3   Journaling Prompt

Journaling Prompt

Think of the work you have done with your students this year.
What did not meet the expectations you had?
Was it "good" but could have been better?
What would benefit from being looked at with colleagues?
What would you have brought to be tuned with a colleague?
What would you have brought to be tuned with a protocol?
Describe the work and come up with a focus question that you might use.

SOURCE: Terry Campanella, adapted from the work of Debra Smith and Fern Tavalin.

Similarly, if PLC membership decides to investigate a collective wondering, the foci for the group's wondering and ideas for framing the wondering are brainstormed at the meeting. Terri uses a *learning community matrix* (Figure 3.5) to initiate dialogue around the formation of a collective wondering. In this activity, PLC members decide on a name for their community based on the work they have done to date. Next, the community completes the K box in the matrix by answering the question, "What do we already *know* as a result of our PLC work to date?" Next, members of the community complete the W box by answering the question, "What do we *want* to know?" Finally, members complete the third P box with a *plan* for finding out what they want to know. After this box is completed, the coach helps translate the plan into the statement of a wondering, and facilitates discussion about the proposed wondering until all PLC members feel comfortable with the question and the direction for their shared inquiry. After the inquiry is completed, the group returns to the matrix and completes the final, L box, stating what members have *learned* as a result of their collective inquiry.

Whether the PLC wondering development meeting is a time when all members of the PLC work to formulate one collective wondering or each individual of the PLC is formulating a personal wondering for exploration, as initial possibilities for wonderings are articulated, the coach facilitates the process of PLC members "playing" with the wondering by taking a *wondering litmus test.*

THE WONDERING LITMUS TEST

Chemists use a litmus test to determine if a substance is an acid or a base. Coaches use this litmus test to determine if the statement of a potential

Figure 3.4   Reflective Guide

REFLECTIVE GUIDE

Learning From Examination of Student/Professional Work

In preparation for our January meeting, please use this guide to:

- Identify a question about your practice.
- Select student/professional work that relates most directly to your question.

1. What questions do I have about my practice as an educator?

2. Which of these questions (from #1) most directly affect student learning? Why?

3. Of the questions generated in #2, which ONE question do I have a passion to learn more about with the help of other colleagues, and do I think most directly affects student learning? **(This is my inquiry question.)**

4. What student/professional work do I have that relates most directly to this question? How does this work relate to my question?

Please bring at least six copies of the work you have identified, along with this completed sheet, to the January meeting.

SOURCE: Terry Campanella, adapted from the work of Debra Smith and Fern Tavalin.

Figure 3.5   Learning Community Matrix

Learning Community Matrix

Community Name: _____ Date Completed: _____

| K
What do we **know** about this community? | W
What do we **want** to know? | P
What is our **plan** for finding out what we want to know? | L
What have we **learned?**
(This is to be completed after we analyze data.) |
|---|---|---|---|
| | | | |
| | | | |

SOURCE: Terry Campanella, adapted from the work of Debra Smith and Fern Tavalin.

wondering for teacher inquiry is worthy of exploration, and if it is articulated in such a way that exploration of the wondering will be the most
valuable it can be for the classroom teacher(s) undertaking the inquiry
journey. The wondering litmus test consists of a series of questions facilitators can pose to themselves or to the group about the wondering
under consideration, and through dialogue and discussion, reframe
and refine a wondering until the individual or group has clearly and
concisely articulated a question that generates excitement, enthusiasm,
and intrigue.

When a teacher articulates a wondering for the first time, it may be
helpful to write the question on a whiteboard or chart paper to begin discussion. Some of the questions a wondering litmus test might include
are illustrated in Figure 3.6 and listed below, followed by stories of how

considering that question helped move an initially articulated wondering through the development phase.

Before proceeding in this chapter, however, it is important to note that these stories are just glimpses into PLC work, and not meant to represent the entire process of wondering development or the evolution of a "perfect" wondering. In the business of teacher inquiry and coaching school-based professional development, there is no such thing as perfection. Rather, the stories are offered as a tool to guide a PLC coach in facilitating the process of representing a teacher's felt tension or dilemma of practice as a question written on the page, and "playing" with the wording, phrasing, and form of the question to help a teacher dig deeper into his or her own proposed inquiry. The questions in the litmus test may be evoked in any order, or some not at all, to help the coach and PLC members "play" with wording, and in the process, get to the heart of teachers' passion for reflection and action. You may also add your own questions to the wondering litmus test.

Is the Wondering Specific?

Pam was the third member of her PLC to share at the group's wondering development meeting. She began, "I'm always thinking about ways to improve my teaching so that I can reach more students and this will be the perfect opportunity to actually follow my 'wonderings' all the way through! I'm constantly changing things but never totally analyze the results of those changes, so I'm really enjoying this PLC work. . . .

"Of course, like everyone here, I sometimes feel like my teaching is drowning in the sea of concern about student performance on our lovely state standardized test. Therefore, I am currently using the computer

Figure 3.6 The Wondering Litmus Test

Take the Wondering Litmus Test

- Is the wondering specific?
- Is the wondering focused on student learning?
- Is the wondering a *real* question (a question whose answer is not known)?
- Is the wondering a question about which the teacher is passionate?
- Is the wondering a "how can I" wondering?
- Is the wondering free of judgmental language?
- Is the wondering focused on the teacher's *own* practice?
- Is the wondering a dichotomous (yes/no) question?
- Is the wondering clear and concise?
- Is your wondering doable?

program provided by the Department of Education to prepare kids for the Florida Comprehensive Assessment Test (FCAT Explorer) every Friday in the classroom. I've been using it since November and really wonder how beneficial it is to my students. I believe this is what I'm going to do my inquiry on. I'm not really sure of how to go about gathering data . . . here are a few of my thoughts. . . . I could survey the students after they take the FCAT and ask them how they think FCAT Explorer helped them prepare. . . . I could monitor on-task time while they are working on the computer. . . . I could analyze the results of their work from a report done by FCAT Explorer. . . . HELP! Am I on the right track? Are these too broad?"

As Pam talked, the coach, Debbi, quickly wrote on a piece of chart paper, "How beneficial is FCAT Explorer?" Debbi initiated the PLC dialogue by pointing at the question and saying, "Pam is interested in understanding the benefits of using FCAT Explorer with her students. She also articulated a wondering about her wondering—is it too broad? What do you think?"

PLC member, Kim, responded, "Well, Pam, I think you have a terrific start here. Performance on FCAT is a topic that I think resonates strongly with everyone in this room." (All members of the PLC nodded in reaction to Kim's statement). "A question that I think about when I look at the wording of your wondering—How beneficial is FCAT Explorer?—is what types of benefits are you looking for from utilizing it? Are you looking for an increase in student confidence taking the FCAT? Increase in student scores on the FCAT? Are there any learning goals associated with your students' use of FCAT Explorer in addition to test-taking skills, familiarity with the test, and building confidence?

After some thought, Pam acknowledged that what she was really after from utilizing FCAT Explorer each Friday afternoon was helping her students develop a familiarity with the test, as well as confidence in taking the test. She refined her wondering statement to be: "What is the relationship between my students' weekly use of FCAT Explorer and their confidence in taking the FCAT?"

PLC Coach, Debbi, continued, "I know another component many teachers have shared with me related to FCAT test preparation is balancing test preparation, the teaching of test-taking skills, (all very important for FCAT success) with other learning experiences. How much test preparation is beneficial to performance on standardized testing? How can I navigate the tension between preparing students for a high-stakes test and other components of my teaching practice? These are conversations I've heard from some teachers, and even conversations we've had in our PLC in the past."

"That's interesting," Pam replied. She paused, thought, and continued, "Maybe what I'm really interested in is exploring the amount of time I spend during the school day focused on preparation for the FCAT and perceived benefits and actual benefits for FCAT performance. It feels like after we return from our break in December that there's a real press to focus on

FCAT preparation and the time I spend on things like FCAT Explorer takes away the time I spend on other learning activities. Certainly preparation for FCAT is important, but I don't think anyone has ever looked at how much time is too much time, if you know what I mean. We just keep being bombarded with more and more FCAT material, and I feel like I better use it all, or I risk poor student performance on the test. I've never really analyzed the value of any of these materials, however. I just pretty much blindly use everything that comes our way.

"Wow, this is really helpful! I'm going to work on the wording of my wondering a bit more now, so I can somehow investigate the different tools and activities I use to prepare my kids for FCAT (including FCAT Explorer), the time I spend on these activities in the classroom, and the value addedness of each preparation strategy for FCAT performance. I'm not exactly sure how I'll do it yet, but perhaps by framing my wondering in this way, I'll be able to more closely scrutinize the ways I'm spending time in my class, and better balance preparation for FCAT with continued learning in my classroom."

● ● ●

In this story, Pam began with a very broad wondering, "How beneficial is FCAT Explorer?" Through careful questions from her coach and members of her PLC, she was pushed to consider more carefully what she meant by "beneficial" and subsequently reworded her wondering to the more specific question, "What is the relationship between my students' weekly use of FCAT Explorer and their confidence in taking the FCAT?" Through further probing from the coach, Pam began to articulate the tension she felt as the time it was taking to prepare her kids for the FCAT was taking time away from engaging her kids in continued learning. By working to make Pam's question more specific, a focus on student learning emerged. Assessing a wondering's focus on student learning is another venue a coach can use to help teachers "play with" the wording of their wonderings.

Is the Wondering Focused on Student Learning?

In her second year as a third grade teacher, Julie Jones chatted with the facilitator of her PLC over lunch on Friday. "I've been thinking about our next PLC meeting on Monday afternoon, and what I want to focus on for my inquiry to share with the group. I'm toying with the idea of doing my inquiry on how to manage the last ten to fifteen minutes of the day. It always seems so hectic and stressful. You know, packing up, answering questions, getting notes to parents in backpacks, organizing the classroom . . . all that kind of stuff. What do you think, and how might I word this to share at our meeting on Monday?"

Linda, the PLC coach, took a bite of her sandwich and pondered Julie's question. "I think this sounds like a wonderful topic for an inquiry that many teachers would be extremely interested in, particularly primary grade teachers! I know the office staff always cringes when we have a new substitute in kindergarten, because they never begin getting the kids ready in time for the bus, especially in the winter when each five-year-old has to be stuffed into their snowsuits, mittens, hat, and boots. When a kindergarten class has a new substitute, there are always bus delays!"

Julie and Linda laughed. Linda continued, "Something that might help fine-tune this inquiry a bit is thinking about *why* you are interested in those last fifteen minutes. For example, are you interested in increasing the efficiency of managing the last fifteen minutes taskwise to shorten the time it takes to get ready to leave? Are you interested in building classroom community goals? As you answer the why question, it will help you think about the wording of your wondering and ways to collect data to answer your question.

Julie responded, "I haven't really thought that deeply about it yet—I just know that those last fifteen minutes don't feel right. I guess I just want my kids and me not to feel so scattered at the end of the day. . . . So, how would something like—How can I increase the efficiency of the last fifteen minutes of the day in my third grade classroom?—be for a wondering?"

Linda grabbed a piece of scrap paper from the table, and jotted down that question. As Linda and Julie considered the wondering on paper, Linda shared her thinking, "This is a great start. Efficiency is really important for managing classroom routines so that the precious instructional time we have as teachers isn't burned away by classroom management. Now that we have your wondering worded on paper, I have a question for you. What might you learn about your students as a result of exploring this wondering?"

Julie was perplexed and intrigued at the same time as she pondered this question. "That's a good question. I can alleviate the stress I feel at the end of the day, but I'm not sure I'll necessarily discover anything about my kids through this wondering. Maybe I don't only want to be efficient, but effective too!"

"Tell me more about what you mean by effective," Linda queried.

"Well, I want to make the most of every minute of the day I have with the kids. I really want to build my classroom as a community, and help my students take responsibility for that sense of community. I also want to milk every academic learning moment there is—I wonder if there's a way to get to a place where the end of the day is not only efficient, but also effective for meeting learning community and academic goals."

Linda returned to the paper and carroted in the words *and effectiveness* so that Julie's wondering now read, "How can I increase the efficiency and effectiveness of the last fifteen minutes of the day in my third grade classroom?" She stated, "This may be a good overarching wondering, that could be fleshed out with some supplemental wonderings that help you focus on your students and their learning during those last fifteen minutes as well."

Julie replied, "I wonder how other primary grade teachers organize the close of their day, and if I can find any books or articles that might help me. If I try some new things, I want to do it with the goal of connecting end of the day routines to social and academic goals for the kids. Is it okay for an inquiry to try some new things and then collect data so that I can understand how they're working?"

"That makes a lot of sense. I see that you are taking your wondering a little deeper. Lets brainstorm some subquestions together." As they thought out loud, Julie added the following to her scrap paper:

- What end of the day routines are already in place and how are they working? How much time do they take?
- What do I hope to accomplish in the last fifteen minutes?
- How do other primary teachers utilize the last fifteen minutes?
- What new structures might I introduce into the last fifteen minutes of the day to connect management to social learning and academic goals for my students?
- How are the newly introduced routines working?

Julie glanced at the clock and realized she had just one minute to get to the cafeteria to pick up her kids, and not aggravate the lunch aide. She quickly whisked out of the teacher's lounge, simultaneously grabbing the paper with her brainstormed wonderings, thanking Linda, and sharing that she was going to play with the wording of her wondering(s) a bit over the weekend and looked forward to the PLC group meeting on Monday!

───────── ●●● ─────────

In this story, in her second year of teaching, Julie began by focusing her wondering exclusively on the efficiency of classroom routines, "How can I increase the efficiency of the last fifteen minutes of the day in my third grade classroom?" Although this focus is natural and developmentally appropriate for a beginning teacher, by posing the question, "What might you learn about your students by exploring this wondering?" coach Linda gently pushed Julie to consider not only management efficiency, but ways management might relate to goals Julie holds for student learning.

Although the target goal for everything one does as a teacher is student learning, sometimes teachers lose sight of their target when immersed in all of the complexity teaching entails. A teacher's target, student learning, is blurred by a number of factors that compete for a teacher's attention. When a coach helps a teacher articulate an explicit connection to student learning within the statement of his or her wondering, the coach is helping the teacher bring the target—student learning—back into focus. Student learning becomes the driving force of the inquiry.

Is the Wondering a *Real* Question (a Question Whose Answer Is Not Known)?

Third grade teacher Lynn was passionate about technology and the meaningful integration of technology into her instruction. It came as no surprise to the members of her PLC when she began sharing about using her latest gadget—an Interwrite Pad. This bluetooth wireless electronic whiteboard comes with software that allows students to be interactive during a lesson. Lynn boasted, "This technology lets me teach from anywhere in the classroom, or sometimes I pass it to a student and let them contribute from their desk."

Jack, the PLC coach interjected, "Okay, Lynn. You know how I am with technology. I'm still using the tried-and-true overhead projector!" (Members of the PLC chuckled, as Jack often poked fun of his own reluctance to incorporate technology into the classroom, but with some support always did end up adapting the latest technology the district had to offer.) "Tell me, what exactly *is* an Interwrite Pad?"

Lynn replied, "Oh Jack, it is truly amazing. You would love it! It looks like a miniature whiteboard, but it interfaces with the computer. As the students write on it, it can be projected on screen for the whole class to see at once. It also allows students to work in groups. You've got to come down to my classroom to see it sometime."

Lynn went on to share that she first introduced the Interwrite Pad into the teaching of reading. She was literally exploding with enthusiasm as she recounted stories of different students in her class and the ways the Interwrite Pad was engaging and motivating them. She ended with the statement, "So my wondering is—How can I effectively use the Interwrite Pad to teach reading?"

Jack, as PLC group facilitator, wrote her wondering on the whiteboard as she stated it. He summarized what Lynn had shared with the group. "So what I hear you saying is that you have recently begun using the Interwrite Pad to teach reading, and all of the students in your class are finding it to be very motivating. You're observing that this tool keeps all learners engaged during reading, and you want to document how well it's working?"

"Well," Lynn responded, "Sort of. I actually purchased the Interwrite Pad because I thought it would be a really powerful tool for all of my students. I was so excited and enthusiastic at the response I was getting from the entire class, until I noticed that my struggling readers didn't seem as engaged as the rest of the class. A technology tool that seemed to be 'Oh, Wow!' at first turned to 'Oh, Bummer' when I noticed my students with severe reading problems begin to disengage during the lesson. This seems to be so counterintuitive to me—I thought the Interwrite Pad would provide a perfect tactile experience for these struggling kiddos."

Referring to the whiteboard with Lynn's initial question written on it, another PLC member commented, "It sounds to me that you already know how to use the Interwrite Pad to effectively teach a reading lesson to the majority of your class. You might want to rephrase your wondering to focus on those learners that are puzzling to you. Maybe something like, 'How do I effectively teach struggling readers using the Interwrite Pad?'"

Jack chimed in, "Or maybe it's not about effectively teaching your struggling readers using the Interwrite Pad, but systematically exploring the reasoning behind your observation that these struggling kids aren't benefiting in the ways you anticipated they would through using this technology. Maybe something like, 'How do struggling readers experience the use of the Interwrite Pad?' Or maybe even broader, 'How do my struggling readers experience reading time in my classroom?' You might be able to get at that through focused observation as well as interviewing your kiddos. Plus maybe looking at their work. If you gain insights into how they are experiencing their struggle with reading, you may gain insights into the Interwrite Pad, and ways you might alter your instruction for these kids to reach them."

Lynn responded, "You're right. I like where this is going! I do know the Interwrite Pad can work wonders, but it's my kids with the severe reading problems I'm puzzled about. My wondering should focus there. I'm going to play with it some more as I design my inquiry and I'll run it by you all when I'm ready. Thanks!"

● ● ●

In this story, Lynn initially thought her wondering focused on effectively using the Interwrite Pad to teach reading. As she talked, however, it became clear that she already knew the answer to that question—she was doing it, and felt really good about it, describing it as "Oh Wow." However, her "Oh Wow" description of using the Interwrite Pad didn't apply to her students with severe reading problems. In Lynn's words, something that was "Oh Wow" went to "Oh Bummer" when she watched struggling readers disengage during instruction. Lynn was truly puzzled by this, and with the help of her coach and PLC members, began to shift the statement of her wondering to focus on something she didn't know the answer to—why her struggling readers were disengaging during instruction that was extremely engaging to every other member of the class.

It is not uncommon for teachers to initially word their wondering as a question they already know the answer to. If they stay on this path, they risk investing time and energy into an inquiry that will merely confirm something they already know, and not lead to any new discoveries about their teaching. Through careful listening, coaches and PLC members can help teachers identify "already know the answer to" wonderings, and reframe and refocus them in more productive and valuable ways.

Is the Wondering a Question About Which the Teacher Is Passionate?

Steve's passion for teaching high school chemistry caught fire with his participation in a PLC at his school. He especially enjoyed interacting with other teachers outside of the science department, and found that listening to their experiences teaching other subject areas (English, Spanish, math, geometry, and biology) offered him a fresh perspective on his own teaching of chemistry. Last year, his PLC members helped Steve craft an inquiry that helped him look deeply at the use of lecture demonstrations to empower student learning. Steve learned a great deal about his practice through engaging in this inquiry, and was even invited to present his research at his state's annual science teacher meeting. This school year, Steve's PLC decided to again support each other in the teacher research they would conduct into their own classrooms. Steve was looking forward to another cycle of inquiry.

Knowing that this PLC not only worked well together, but also enjoyed each other's company, PLC facilitator and English teacher, Greg, suggested that the group meet Friday afternoon at 4:00 at a local bar to share and discuss their potential questions for exploration through inquiry. Greg affectionately referred to this meeting as, "Our Wondering Happy Hour." The group agreed that it would be a nice, relaxed way to get moving on the research.

In between chicken wings and sips of beer, group members each took a turn sharing questions. Greg looked at Steve, "We haven't heard from you yet. What are you thinking about for this year?"

Steve began, "I've been thinking about my assessment strategies, especially the tests I give. I'm thinking of doing something focused on my students' performance on these tests . . . maybe do an item analysis, or something like that."

Greg noticed from Steve's body language and tone of voice that the same enthusiasm evident throughout Steve's inquiry the previous year was not present. Greg invited Steve to elaborate on his thinking, "Tell me more."

"The tests just don't feel right to me, so it might help to analyze their content."

Greg continued, "What would you expect to learn about your students from this inquiry?"

"I'm not sure what I'd learn about my students from analyzing the tests, but I can tell you something about the students I teach. There's a small group of kids that rely extremely heavily on my extra-help sessions.

Because they know I offer these sessions, as the school requires us to do, they don't pay attention when I introduce a concept to be tested in class—instead they figure they can pick it up in the extra-help session."

Greg noticed Steve was becoming more and more animated as he talked about the extra-help sessions. Steve continued, "Often in chemistry, my students are overwhelmed with the complexity of learning such an abstract science. They often enter my class having heard stories from their parents about the horrors of college chemistry classes. Many have notions that chemistry is something that will be impossible for them to learn. I, as a chemistry teacher, realize that the subject will be more easily understood by some students than others. Many of my students honestly need help outside of the normal class in order to achieve an acceptable grade. Help sessions are a place where students can get the help they need. Yet, what I have noticed is that many of these students rely on these out-of-class help sessions to be a place where they can learn the concepts that I have already taught in class itself. As a result, some of my students are off task during class because they feel like they can learn the material in the help session anyhow. Why do they need to pay attention during class?"

Greg responded, "It seems to me that the tests themselves are not what you are really interested in exploring, but the help sessions to prepare students for the test."

"Yes," Steve replied, "that's it. More specifically, I would like to examine my students' perceptions of help sessions. I feel like maybe a different perspective would be beneficial both to them as students and to myself as their teacher. I think that help sessions should be better termed *office hours*. Students should come to these office hours to seek answers to questions, not to be taught concepts that have already been covered in class."

Greg grabbed his notepad and said, "Let's jot down those ideas before we lose them." On the pad, Greg wrote the phrases, "Understanding Student Perceptions of Help Session," and "Getting a Different Perspective on Help Sessions." Steve worked some more on that paper, playing with questions to frame his inquiry. When he left the happy hour that evening, he read through the scribbling on his notepad:

- What is the most productive way to structure afterschool help?
- What are students' perceptions and expectations for extra help?
- How does one create a student driven versus teacher driven afterschool session?
- What is the relationship between misbehavior during class and attendance at afterschool help?
- What skills do my students need to take charge of their extra help?
- What is the chemistry skill level of my students who seek help outside of class?
- Are these help times increasing the knowledge of my chemistry students?

Steve believed he had a great start to wondering development, and was excited to get this inquiry underway!

●●●

In this story, the coach used keen observation skills. Greg could ascertain through Steve's body language, tone of voice, and facial expressions what Steve was and was not passionate about exploring. Through inviting Steve to continue talking ("Tell me more") and gently posing some questions that helped Steve delve deeper into his thinking ("What would you expect to learn about your students through this inquiry?"), Greg created a space for Steve's true passion (the extra-help session) to emerge in the natural progression of his talk.

One of the most important factors in coaching inquiry is ensuring that a question is one that a teacher owns and is truly passionate about exploring. Completing the cycle of inquiry is hard work, and if a teacher isn't truly passionate about a wondering, he or she risks losing the commitment to sustain an inquiry over time. With patience, careful listening, and questioning, effective coaches can draw out the burning questions about practice that reside in the heart of every teacher.

Is the Wondering a "How Can I" Wondering?

Beverly had been teaching in the primary grades at her elementary school for twenty-five years and attributed her involvement in the formation and development of a primary grade PLC at her school to a renewed passion for teaching. Her group consisted of the three first and three second grade teachers in her building. They were a diverse group, but all shared a passion for young learners. The primary PLC group met every first Wednesday of the month, on early release days. Bev felt fortunate that her district released the children one hour and fifteen minutes early each Wednesday at the elementary level to afford teachers planning and professional development time. The primary grades PLC was facilitated by Sandra, the reading coach at Bev's school.

At the previous meeting, the group decided that it wished to fine-tune and refine the implementation of a guided reading program that was instituted at the school the previous year. Guided reading is one component of the shared reading block during which the teacher provides support for small, flexible groups of beginning readers. The program consists of self-selected reading, shared reading, writing, and working with words. By reading text that is unfamiliar to them, students learn to use reading strategies, such as context clues, letter and sound knowledge, and syntax or word structure. The overarching objective of guided reading is for students to use these strategies independently on their way to becoming fluent, skilled readers.

Two summers ago, the primary grade teachers had attended a summer institute on guided reading, and spent the following school year in their PLC group using text-based protocols to do further reading on this approach to teaching, as well as protocols to examine student work in their primary classrooms. Some PLC members also shared dilemmas they encountered as they translated guided reading strategies into practice.

Borne out of the previous year's PLC discussions on guided reading, this year, as reading coach and PLC facilitator, Sandra suggested that the group might focus on studying various guided reading strategies to develop deeper understandings of how they play out in practice. Group members agreed that "Guided Reading Strategies" would be a great focus for the year, and decided that each member of the PLC would select a strategy that was of particular interest to him or her, and develop an action research question to explore in his or her own classroom this school year. They would use their PLC meetings to talk about their individual research, and in addition learn a great deal about guided reading by looking across the individual, but related work each PLC member was undertaking.

Beverly eagerly looked forward to their next meeting, during which she was going to share her "slice" of the PLC's collective inquiry into guided reading—the word wall. Word walls are a systematically organized collection of words displayed in large letters on a wall or other large display place in the classroom. In anticipation of her next PLC meeting, Bev e-mailed Sandra:

> I decided to focus on the literacy centers in my classroom and, more specifically, word walls. I do not feel I make much use of my word wall and the kids do not seem to be interactive with it, yet I keep hearing the words of the guided reading trainer in my head over and over again, "The word wall is a tool, not a display." I guess where I am leading is: How can I use my word wall in a literacy center to make it more meaningful for my students? Do you think this will work or do I need to narrow it down even more? This week I started with prefixes pre-, re-, and un-, and had the students partner read and then find words with these prefixes and add those words to the word wall. The students seemed to like it, but how do I follow up to make sure it really is useful? I am just brainstorming and would appreciate any thoughts from you. Thanks!—Beverly

Sandra was excited when she read Bev's e-mail. As reading coach and PLC facilitator, she wanted to gently push the PLC members in their inquiries beyond the development and implementation of strategies, to focus on the implications of implementing the new strategies, and she believed Bev was headed in that direction. She responded:

> Hi Beverly—I think your focus on word walls will be fantastic for our group! It seems to me that many teachers in our building have

word walls displayed, but are unsure of how to make them useful and interactive. Your inquiry can really be informative to not just our PLC members, but the teachers in the intermediate grades as well. When I read your wondering, the first thing I noticed was that you began with the phrase, "How can I?" It seems since our PLC is focusing on the reading curriculum in the primary grades this year, we are all starting to phrase our related wonderings with the words "How can I?" For example, I talked with Marge yesterday and she was interested in exploring, "How can I use partner reading with first graders?" While "How can I . . . " phrased questions are wonderful starting points for inquiries, if we stop here, I fear that our work may become purely the development of lesson plans and activities without systematic study of what was developed. I think this is what you are doing with the development and implementation of your first activity of having students look for words using the prefixes pre-, re-, and un-, and adding those words to the word wall. The development and implementation of new activities is important and wonderful work, and we did a lot of that last year as we were implementing guiding reading for the first time in our classrooms. Yet, in your statement, "The students seemed to like it but how do I follow up to make sure it really is useful?" you are realizing that it is the focus on what is learned about the development and implementation of activities that will deepen our thinking and teaching, not the development of new activities in and of themselves. To be sure we focus on what is learned from implementing new strategies, I'm thinking that if we all begin with a "How can I" phrased wondering, it might also be helpful to formulate a companion wondering that leads us beyond the lessons/activities we develop to what we are learning about our kids, the guided reading curriculum, and/or ourselves as teachers as a result of developing and implementing guiding reading strategies. What do you think? —Sandra

Sandra hit the send button, shut down her computer, gathered her belongings, and left for home. When Sandra checked her e-mail the next morning, she read the following response from Bev:

Sandra—Thanks for your reply. I see what you are saying—"How Can I" wonderings often begin with developing activities to make something happen (In my case using the prefixes pre-, re-, un- and having students partner read, then find words with these prefixes to add to the word wall). The next step is to implement the strategy and "study" how it works. One thing I might do is take notes as I implement strategies such as the one I developed on prefixes. I also could interview students (just informally, of course, in first grade) after a strategy is utilized to see their perceptions of its usefulness.

I might ask you, as the reading coach, to come in and observe my students in action as I implement my strategies—maybe other members of our PLC might even be interested in some peer coaching. I'm just doing some brainstorming here of ways I might collect data to gain insights into my wondering.

Developing some companion wonderings to my "How can I" wondering might help me continue to focus on what I am learning about implementing the new word wall strategies rather than just the development of the strategies themselves. Here are some ideas I'm playing with that I'll share at our next PLC meeting:

Overarching Wondering: How can I use my word wall in a literacy center to make it more meaningful to my students?

Subquestions:

How am I currently using my word wall?

How do other elementary teachers utilize word walls in their classrooms?

What strategies might increase the word wall's usefulness and the ways it engages my learners?

What is the relationship between the new strategies I employ and my students' learning?

Thanks again, Sandra! I really appreciate your help. —Bev

———————————— ● ● ● ————————————

In this story, Sandra and Beverly's e-mail exchange helps both of them focus as much on the learning that is happening as a result of trying new strategies for using a word wall as they are focusing on the development and implementation of the new strategies for using word walls themselves. When a teacher-researcher begins her wondering with the common phrase, "How can I?" there is a possibility that the inquiry will never actually develop into an inquiry, but get stuck in the development and implementation phase of the process. Sometimes creative teachers, especially, become so excited about new strategies and techniques that appear fun to students, they stop at the implementation phase, never systematically exploring the ways something that appears to be enjoyable for kids contributes to academic learning. In the case of "How can I?" wonderings, it is often productive for the coach to guide the teacher to focus on the relationship between the new thing they are trying and student learning. Coaches might pose the question, "What do you hope your students will learn from this activity?"

In addition, it is often fruitful to try adding some companion wonderings to a "How can I?" wondering, as Beverly began to do in this case.

Is the Wondering Free of Judgmental Language?
And, Is the Wondering Focused on the Teacher's *Own* Practice?

Fifth grade teacher Ashley and her colleague teaching in the third grade, Marissa, decided to team on a collaborative inquiry as they both shared a frustration with their current report card system, and hoped to be a catalyst for change. Their elementary school had worked hard over the years to provide solid feedback to parents on student progress, and each quarter, a detailed report of student performance on various measures was sent home. Ashley and Marissa believed a report on various assessments helped portray where the students were at in relationship to grade-level goals and expectations, as well as where they were at in relationship to their own individual progress over time. However, in addition to this detailed report, teachers in the elementary school also assigned a traditional letter grade to each student. Ashley and Marissa wondered why. With only ten minutes left in their PLC's wondering development meeting, Ashley and Marissa were the last two teachers to share their idea for an inquiry. Marissa began, "I know we are short on time, so we'll be brief. As teachers, you know we all report student progress using a traditional grading system—the assignment of letter grades. Ashley and I would like to explore alternative methods of communicating student progress to all stakeholders. We feel that perceptions of letter grades are varied and may not accurately convey true development."

"I know what you mean," shared PLC member Brian, "I think letter grades should represent student effort on classroom assignments, so I developed a rubric on work ethic, and I mostly use that to determine a student's grade. Sometimes it causes problems, though, when one of my students who is testing below grade level on some of our assessments, brings home an A. The parents don't understand."

"Exactly!" Marissa and Ashley chimed in at the same time.

"Wow, that's a brave inquiry undertaking," shared another teacher in their group. "You know you could potentially hit a lot of hot buttons with that one!"

"We know," Ashley responded, "and that's why we need some help in framing this. We obviously have some real opinions on this subject, and we want to explore it openly. We also don't want to cause a ruckus, if you know what I mean."

"We are nearing the end of our meeting time," PLC facilitator, Donna, shared.

"Could we meet with you sometime in the next week to discuss this some more?"

"Sure," responded Donna. "Let's find a time after our meeting." Donna ended the PLC meeting with an "Aha and Questions" reflection sheet.

The following Wednesday, Donna, Ashley, and Marissa met in Marissa's classroom after school. Marissa printed out the list of questions she and Ashley had brainstormed together after their previous PLC meeting. "Donna, we really need some help. It just seems like this is so big, and we're not sure where to focus. Here's what we have so far." They viewed the printout of questions together:

- How do teachers accurately assign a grade?
- What is the difference between accurate assessment and actual grades?
- Does the traditional method of assigning letter grades provide the most accurate portrait of a student's progress?
- What alternative methods are available that may better convey student progress?

Ashley continued, "What we were thinking was that we would search into the history of our current system to understand the continuing use of letter grades. We will gather data from all stakeholders to better understand perceptions of letter grades by giving out surveys. Additionally, we will research alternative methods of communicating student progress and also review current literature regarding traditional verses alternative grading systems. We just aren't sure where to go. It seems big. It seems that the topic could be touchy, and we know we have strong opinions. We want to be open-minded, but how?"

"Okay," Donna replied. "Give me a minute. Let me just look at your questions and think for a little bit." Donna looked at the sheet of paper, did some underlining, and jotted down a few notes. She proceeded, "You've got a lot going on here and a lot to think about. Let's start by looking at the questions you brainstormed. One thing I noticed was the word *accurate*. That word is all over the place. It appears in your first three questions in one form or another. Tell me what you mean by the word *accurate*."

Marissa spoke, "I think what we mean is a *real* representation of the student."

Donna queried, "What does that mean to you?"

Marissa continued, "Well to me it has to include a reflection of effort. But I know for some teachers that's not what it means, and they spend a lot of time constructing ways to assign a grade to a student using number grades on class assignments, and for what? What does that really show?"

Ashley added, "And the parents and the students don't always see things the way you intended as a teacher. It's a real mess."

"So," Donna said, "In your own minds you have a strong view of what should be, and this view of what should be is the way you are defining the word *accurate* in your wondering statements."

Ashley and Marissa looked at each other and laughed. "I guess we should get rid of the word *accurate*, huh? Pretty judgmental?"

"The word *accurate* does have some value judgment inherent in it. As I listen to you talk, what I think I hear you being troubled by is varying perceptions teachers and parents have about what constitutes the letter grade of A, B, C, and so on. Is this *accurate?*—no pun intended!" Marissa and Ashley giggled at Donna's play on words.

"Yes, that's right, and the students too! What if we framed a wondering statement something like—How do student, parent, and teacher perceptions affect the way grades are interpreted?—Is that better? You know, opening ourselves up for this inquiry, and not clouding our inquiry with our opinion?"

Donna wrote down this question as Ashley spoke. She spoke the question again slowly out loud as she and the two teachers considered it, "How do student, parent, and teacher perceptions affect the way grades are interpreted?—I think that's getting there. Tell, me, though, how will you collect data on this question?"

Ashley spoke, "I guess we'd survey parents and other teachers—you know, something like what does the letter grade of A mean to you; what does the letter grade of B mean to you?"

"We'd have to think about that more, and also be careful about how we worded the surveys. I wonder if we'd really get many turned in too."

"Hmmm," Donna paused and thought. "Okay, let me ask you a question. If you were to send out surveys to teachers and parents to get at their perceptions, what would you learn about your own practice?"

There was a pause, as Ashley and Marissa carefully considered this question. Ashley spoke first: "Nothing really, I guess. I think we'd end up just confirming what we already know. Letter grades mean something different to everyone, and we'd probably open up a can of worms."

Donna continued, "What if you turned the focus of your gaze from looking outside to other teachers and parents at large, and looking inside of yourselves and your practice with grading."

"Tell me more," Marissa said.

"What if you looked at your own grading practices? It sounds like you are uncomfortable with the discrepancy that sometimes appears between the letter grade you assign to certain learners, and their accompanying report on various assessments when they don't match. Have you ever looked systematically at these cases and what you can learn from them? Maybe the two of you can sit down together and look at all of your recent report cards, selecting the ones where students received a letter grade of A, but a below grade-level rating on some of the assessments you use, or a student received a letter grade of B or C, but is performing at or above grade level on assessments, and investigate these cases in depth. How do these parents make sense of the discrepancy?"

"I like that," Marissa said, "But if we go this route, then where does the change part come in? Ashley and I are really interested in igniting a discussion among our faculty about our grading system. If we just focus on ourselves, how does that happen?"

"It happens through the sharing of your inquiry and what you learned as you looked deeply at your own students and their parents. This sharing will generate discussion, but the discussion emerges from your practice, not your assessment of other's practice."

Marissa responded, "That makes sense. The discussion might still lead to a heated debate, but when we focus on ourselves rather than others, it's less likely we'll be threatening to others, and come off like we're trying to impose something, when really we're not. We truly do want to resolve the tension we're feeling between assigning the letter grades along with our assessment report, and I'm pretty sure other teachers are feeling this tension as well. We'll have much to share with other teachers in our school by looking at our *own* students and parents and the ways they make sense of letter grades and our whole reporting system. That's a great way to get started. Ashley and I will work a bit on framing our inquiry in this way, and we'll bring a question to our next PLC meeting to share with the group. I can't wait to get started. Thanks!"

● ● ●

In this story, Ashley and Marissa had a strong opinion about the assignment of letter grades in their elementary school—there was no need to assign letter grades! Their strong opinion crept into their wondering statements. By calling attention to the word *accurate* and inviting Ashley and Marissa to speak about what that word meant to them, Donna created a space for the strong opinion Ashley and Marissa held to be articulated. Once articulated, the formation of the opinion could be explored for the issues that surrounded it (varying perceptions held by teachers and parents of what a letter grade means). At this point, the phrasing of the wondering evolved to focus on the issue (differing perceptions), rather than on a judgment made by Ashley and Marissa about what constituted accurate grade reporting. As they worked with Donna to rephrase, reword, and reframe their wondering, they discovered more about their own thoughts and subjectivities, and how to keep those in check as they proceeded with their inquiry.

A key to helping Marissa and Ashley consider their own thoughts and the roles they play in teacher inquiry occurred when Donna posed the question, "If you were to send out surveys to teachers and parents to get at their perceptions, what would you learn about your own practice?" The posing of this question created a critical juncture in the design of the inquiry. Marissa and Ashley realized they were focusing outside of themselves, rather than looking inside their own classrooms. They both had the instinct that their wondering didn't feel quite right, and could create a "ruckus," in Ashley's words, but didn't quite know why. Once Donna helped them turn their focus from teachers and parents across the whole school to themselves and the parents of the children in their classroom, Ashley and Marissa felt much more comfortable exploring their passion—letter grades, without alienating other teachers in the building, or potentially agitating parents. They realized that a sound, systematic study of their own experiences with letter grading could provide rich data necessary to provoke discussion facultywide, a much healthier way to serve as a catalyst for school change than designing a study that collected data from others to prove a point.

Is the Wondering a Dichotomous (Yes/No) Question? Is the Wondering Clear and Concise? And, Is the Wondering Doable?

Elementary school principal, Marion, and five of her faculty members met regularly to reflect on the teaching and learning that was occurring in their school building for all members of the community—students, teachers, and administrators. Through the process of using protocols to examine student and educator work, they uncovered and addressed problems and took action to address them. The group was facilitated by Adam, a veteran fourth grade teacher who had been through the NSRF's intensive weeklong training on PLCs three years earlier.

About to embark on a new school year, teachers reported to work one full week before the students after summer vacation and were busy preparing for the arrival of their new class of students. During this preplanning week, Marion called her PLC together to look at their students' results on standardized test scores from the previous school year. Along with Marion, all members of the PLC concluded that they really needed to focus on the bottom quartile of students in their school, and could use the process of action research to make a difference for this population.

Marion shared with Adam and the group, "I've been thinking about this a lot over the summer, and I'm also thinking of a lot of initiatives we have ongoing in our building. I played around with a question that might guide our PLC this year." She handed out a paper with the following words typed across the top:

> Will focusing on the lowest student quartile through teacher culture awareness, mentoring, progress monitoring, intervention by the reading teacher, and the afterschool program be sufficient to raise our percent making AYP (adequate yearly progress) in reading from 47% to 65%?

There was a pause as members of the PLC silently read and considered the wondering statement, and then Marion queried, "Is this too wordy, or is it even where we should be headed?"

Adam began the dialogue, "Marion, thank you so much for getting us started! This actually comes at a great time—I just finished reading an article about teacher and principal research in the Madison, Wisconsin, Metropolitan School District. The article shares ideas for what they believe makes a good action research question. I think we can learn a lot from this article. Among other things, the authors believe that good action research questions are clear and concise, are 'doable,' and require a more complex answer than yes or no (Caro-Bruce & McCreadie, 1994). I think we should play with this research question with these three things in mind. To start, how might we rephrase this question so it is not stated as a dichotomous question?"

PLC member Rita gave it a try, "How about something like: What role does teacher culture awareness, mentoring, progress monitoring, reading teacher intervention, and afterschool program participation play in raising the AYP of our lowest student quartile?"

Adam wrote the question on the whiteboard as Rita spoke. He stepped back and looked at what he had written and responded, "I think that's good. Now it reads as an open-ended question. By carefully wording questions so they are open-ended, we open ourselves up to frame the design of our research to uncover lots of possibilities. When a question is posed in a dichotomous fashion, we force the design of our research to fit into narrow categories."

Marion replied, "Okay, I see that. But I still think the question is really wordy—not clear and concise like that article shares."

Adam responded, "Well, what if we broke that question down further into an overarching wondering with subquestions. Would that make it more clear and concise?"

All members of the PLC agreed that this was a good plan and contributed to the discussion for ideas on how to "pare down" the wondering on the whiteboard. After lots of crossing out and erasing, their discussion led to the following revision of Rita's question that Adam inscribed on the whiteboard for all members of the group to view:

Overarching Wondering: What actions can our faculty take to improve reading achievement of our lowest quartile students?

Sub-Wonderings:

- ○ What is the relationship between teacher culture awareness and raising the adequate yearly progress (AYP) of our lowest quartile?
- ○ What is the relationship between progress monitoring and raising the AYP of our lowest quartile?
- ○ What is the relationship between mentoring and raising the AYP of our lowest quartile?
- ○ What is the relationship between reading teacher intervention and raising the AYP of our lowest quartile?
- ○ What is the relationship between afterschool program participation and raising the AYP of our lowest student quartile?

○ How do our lowest quartile students experience and benefit from engagement with each of these strategies (teacher culture awareness, progress monitoring, mentoring, intervention, afterschool programs)?

The group all agreed that they were making progress, but Rita expressed that it still didn't feel quite right to her. "The process of breaking down this wondering has helped me realize how many initiatives we are participating in. No wonder our faculty was feeling so overwhelmed and stressed at the end of the previous school year. Morale was low. I think we should consider the doability of this research—are we trying to do too much all at once? If we attempt to do too much all at once, can we really do anything well? And if we end up not really doing anything well, how can we get good data to understand how various initiatives are working? If we do too much all at once, we'll only drag ourselves down. We ought to consider this before we proceed."

All members of the PLC nodded in agreement. As it was nearing 4:00 PM, Adam drew attention to the clock and reminded everyone that one of their ground rules was that they always started and ended on time, and they were scheduled to end in five minutes. Through discussion, the group decided that it shared a commitment to focus on the bottom quartile of students this school year, but needed to work further on framing the question and research plan. Adam agreed to look through his book of protocols and find one that might help accomplish this goal at their next meeting.

— ●●● —

In this story, all members of the PLC are working to determine one collective school improvement wondering to explore together. When this happens, it is not uncommon for a wondering to become so large, it is impossible to explore well. It is also not uncommon in this case for the wording of a wondering to become bogged down with a good deal of technical jargon, making it difficult to get a handle on. As coach, Adam skillfully leads PLC members through the process of teasing apart the wondering, and in the process, the group becomes uncomfortable with the number of initiatives it is currently implementing. This, in and of itself, is a valuable learning experience for the PLC.

Sometimes the process of wondering development leads to interesting (and potentially tough to face) discoveries by a teaching team. An effective coach acknowledges these discoveries, and creates a time and a space to examine them more deeply.

LOOKING ACROSS THE LITMUS TEST QUESTIONS AND STORIES

Each of the coaches portrayed in these stories were skilled in facilitating the development of a wondering. A common element across all coaches was their ability to listen carefully and patiently as the teachers they were coaching in the inquiry process gave voice, perhaps for the first time, to a dilemma, problem, issue, or tension in their practice. This articulated dilemma served as a springboard to formulate and state a question for exploration. Once the question was formulated, coach and teacher-inquirer "unpacked" the question together through spoken or written dialogue.

The coaches in this chapter took seven distinct actions in their dialogue with teachers to spur continued talk about the proposed wondering and, in the process, help the inquirer clarify thinking and design an inquiry that would be meaningful to both the teacher and other professionals. These seven actions are summarized in Figure 3.7. The first two actions capture the types of questions the coaches pose to the teachers—clarifying and probing. A clarifying question occurs when a coach needs the answer to a factual question in order to better understand the teacher's inquiry. For example, in the Interwrite Pad inquiry, coach Jack asked Lynn, "What exactly *is* an Interwrite Pad?" By asking clarifying questions, the coach helps the teacher-inquirer share information that may be useful to the coach and other members of the PLC as they consider the teacher's wondering.

Likewise, a probing question occurs when a coach poses a question that causes teachers to reflect on their practice in relationship to the wondering they are proposing. An example of a probing question occurred in the classroom management inquiry when Linda asked Julie, "What might you learn about your students as a result of exploring this wondering?" Some examples of additional probing questions coaching might pose to facilitate teacher thinking about a proposed wondering appear in Figure 3.8.

The next three actions in Figure 3.7 are not questions at all, but intentional statements that coaches make to move dialogue along. A declarative statement occurs when a coach expresses his or her own state of mind or thought in relationship to what the teacher-researcher has just said. For example, in the FCAT Explorer inquiry, Debbi made a direct statement about a thought that occurred to her as Pam pondered out loud on the subject of her reasoning for using FCAT Explorer:

> I know another component many teachers have shared with me related to FCAT test preparation is balancing test preparation, the teaching of test-taking skills, (all very important for FCAT success) with other learning experiences. How much test preparation is beneficial to performance on standardized testing? How can I navigate the tension between preparing students for a high-stakes test and other components of my teaching practice? These are conversations I've heard from some teachers, and even conversations we've had in our PLC in the past.

Figure 3.7   Actions Taken by Coaches During Wondering Discussions

Type of Action	Definition of Action	Example
Clarifying Questions	Coach poses a factual question he or she or PLC members might need an answer to in order to understand the teacher's proposed inquiry.	"What exactly *is* an Interwrite Pad?"
Probing Questions	Coach poses a question that causes teachers to reflect on their practice in relationship to the wondering they are proposing.	"What might you learn about your students as a result of exploring this wondering?"
Declarative Statement	Coach expresses his or her own state of mind or thought in relationship to what the teacher researcher has just said.	"I know another component many teachers have shared with me related to FCAT test preparation is balancing test preparation, the teaching of test-taking skills, (all very important for FCAT success) with other learning experiences."
Reflective Statement	Coach rephrases something the teacher inquirer has just said, giving it an exact and economical sense.	"So what I hear you saying is that you have recently begun using the Interwrite Pad to teach reading, and all of the students in your class are finding it to be very motivating."
Invitation to Elaborate	Coach invites a teacher-researcher to elaborate on his or her thinking.	"Tell me more."
Deliberate Silence	Coach deliberately says nothing at all for some time after a teacher completes a comment.	Pause a few seconds to create think time.
Humor	Coach interjects a funny story related to the inquiry, makes a play on words, or other humorous action to invoke laughter from the group.	Linda paints a picture of an inexperienced substitute kindergarten teacher trying desperately to stuff eighteen five-year-olds into mittens, snowsuits, and boots in order to make it to the buses on time.

Figure 3.8   Probing Questions

Sample Probing Questions

- What might you learn about your students as a result of exploring this wondering?
- What difference might exploring this wondering make in your classroom practice?
- What potential impact will the insights you gain from this inquiry have on you?
- What potential impact will the insights you gain from this inquiry have on your students?
- What potential impact will the insights you gain from this inquiry have on your pedagogy?
- What potential impact will the insights you gain from this inquiry have on the school?

When a coach makes a declarative statement, the teacher-inquirer has the option of accepting or rejecting the coach's declaration, and often speaks elaboratively in acceptance or rejection of that statement. As the teacher speaks, he or she often brings clarity to the proposed inquiry. In the FCAT Explorer case, in response to Debbi's declarative statement, Pam realized she was interested in more than the connection between her students' use of FCAT Explorer and their confidence in taking the test. Rather, she wanted to measure the time she was spending on FCAT review and the time she spent on new learning activities during FCAT season. She wished to discover the value of a number of different FCAT preparation materials she used and ascertain what (and how much of each) contributed to better test performance. She wished to systematically explore how to balance FCAT prep with normal teaching activities. As Pam responded to Debbi's declarative statement, her inquiry was taken to a deeper level.

A reflective statement occurs when the coach rephrases something the teacher-inquirer has just said, giving it an exact and economical sense. A coach forms a reflective statement with such beginning clauses as "I get from what you are saying that . . . " or "So you think that. . . . " Returning to the Interwrite Pad Inquiry, Jack used a reflective statement to summarize Lynn's talk:

> So what I hear you saying is that you have recently begun using the Interwrite Pad to teach reading, and all of the students in your class are finding it to be very motivating. You're observing that this tool keeps all learners engaged during reading, and you want to document how well it's working.

When a coach paraphrases what a teacher-inquirer has just shared, the reflective statement becomes a mirror for the inquirer to examine his or her own ideas as they come out of another's mouth. Hearing what he or she has just said paraphrased by another person often leads to the inquirer offering clarification remarks. In response to Jack's reflective statement, Lynn offered:

> Well, sort of. I actually purchased the Interwrite Pad because I thought it would be a really powerful tool for all of my students. I was so excited and enthusiastic about the response I was getting from the entire class, until I noticed that my struggling readers didn't seem as engaged as the rest of the class.

This act of clarification led Lynn to get to the heart of her dilemma—struggling readers. The act of offering a clarifying statement often leads the teacher-researcher to reveal something more about his or her practice. This revelation can have important implications for a teacher's wondering.

An invitation to elaborate occurs when the coach invites a teacher-researcher to elaborate on his or her thinking. This can be very simple to accomplish, as in the chemistry extra-help inquiry when coach Greg said to Steve, "Tell me more." As Steve continued to speak, a true passion for a wondering was revealed. A coach can also use an invitation to elaborate to probe a teachers' thinking. This is often accomplished by inviting teachers to elaborate more on the meaning they hold for a particular word in their wondering statement, as in the classroom management inquiry when Linda stated, "Tell me more about what you mean by *effective*," and in the letter grade inquiry, when Donna stated, "Tell me what you mean by the word *accurate*." In both of these cases, elaborating on the meaning they held for a specific word led the teachers to dig deeper into their proposed inquiry.

The sixth action a coach can take is really not an action at all, but the absence of an action that takes the form of deliberate, intentional silence. The coach deliberately says nothing at all for some time after a teacher completes a comment. Sometimes, the coach makes the pause for silence explicit as in the letter grade inquiry when Donna stated, "Give me a minute. Let me just look at your questions and think for a little bit." Sometimes, the coach just allows natural silences to happen without interjecting a comment. For example, in the lowest student quartile inquiry, immediately following Marion's presentation of her wondering, coach Adam allowed the PLC members think time: "There was a pause as members of the PLC silently read and considered the wondering statement." Although silence is often perceived as uncomfortable, a skilled coach intentionally uses silence to allow all members of the PLC needed think time before proceeding with the discussion.

A final action a coach can take throughout wondering development may not necessarily contribute to the evolution of a wondering, but helps relax a conversation that can often become intense as teachers voice dilemmas of practice. This final action is providing humor. According to Roland Barth (1990):

Humor is sorely lacking in this profession, in textbooks and educational writing, in research, in state departments, in universities— and in schools. Yet, humor, like risk taking and diversity, is highly related to learning and the development of intelligence, not to mention quality of life. And humor can be a glue that binds an assorted group of individuals into a community. People learn and grow and survive through humor. We should make an effort to elicit and cultivate it, rather than ignore, thwart, or merely tolerate it. (p. 170)

Humor appears throughout the coaching stories in this chapter. Linda and Julie laugh when Linda paints a picture of inexperienced substitute teachers in kindergarten trying desperately to get the five-year-olds ready for bus dismissal during the winter months and the resulting bus delays. Members of the PLC chuckle as Jack pokes fun of his own reluctance to integrate technology into instruction. Marissa and Ashley giggle at Donna's play on the word *accurate* used in their wondering statement and used by Donna to see if her understanding of Marissa and Ashley's inquiry is correct:

As I listen to you talk, what I think I hear you being troubled by is varying perceptions teachers and parents have about what constitutes the letter grade of A, B, C, and so on. Is this *accurate?*—no pun intended!

The work of an inquiry-oriented learning community is difficult, and can even be exhausting at times. The interjection of humor helps all members of the PLC relax, build rapport with each other, and take a momentary break from the great complexity inherent in teaching.

From reading and analyzing each of the stories shared in this chapter and delineating seven distinct actions coaches take in their facilitation of wondering discussions, you may be feeling overwhelmed as a coach! Yet, take heart in the fact that all of the coaches portrayed in this chapter find great joy in their work, as we believe you will as well. Many facilitators we have worked with have articulated that the process of coaching a wondering has renewed and reenergized their passion for the teaching profession. To exemplify, and to inspire, we end this chapter with an e-mail correspondence we received from one of these facilitators, our colleague and friend, Darby Delane:

Hi, Nancy and Diane,

I have become very hooked on helping people articulate their wonderings. While naming a wondering can be empowering for the person I am helping, the process has come to be a very empowering experience for ME. The way I do it with people has come to follow a particular path—each one always different, of course, but usually with the same sort of benchmarks. If you want a metaphor (and I know it's overused, but it is perfect), I feel just like a midwife. These wonderings are precious and, as embryos, they develop and define over time. Getting people to become conscious of that development—being there to help what was previously unconscious become articulated into language in a way that names and problematizes our experiences fills me with hope and awe for the potential power we have as teachers.

As far as the benchmarks of this experience for me are concerned, it usually starts by my reaching into a teacher's heart, into the place where she is uncomfortable, but not willing to go by herself, since it is counterintuitive and can potentially increase a sense of disequilibrium. As she is already overwhelmed, she does not want to increase this discomfort by attending to those felt difficulties. For some the degree of ambivalence in doing this is more intense than others. I try to help create a safe place just to be plain rotten for a brief time—to vent and complain, or be absolutely confused with no answers at all. We can do this in writing through dialogue journal and e-mail, orally one-on-one, and sometimes as "witnesses to dialogue" that have occurred in learning community meetings. I have had teachers tell me that while they didn't want to articulate their own felt difficulties at one of our meetings, it was tremendously freeing for them to witness mine, and those of others willing to voice them. They were able to practice through us and take that courage to their own dilemmas in order to craft a wondering.

It goes on from there. As we problematize our felt difficulties, we begin to coconstruct language that names them in a way that just feels so satisfying—the wondering is born. There is nothing like seeing that previously nonverbal, disorienting irritation come to form and be named on the page in a way that seems workable—doable—maybe even solvable—but even if it isn't solvable, it is manageable. We can do something about it. We can create a plan to investigate and collect data, bring out the raw material necessary to analyze and make an action plan. Self-efficacy goes through the roof, and it doesn't even matter what the outcome is at that point. We are acting upon our worlds in a way that crystallizes our visions for teaching— in a way that makes us feel authentic again—and not alone!

I want to be that safe place for the teachers I work with to practice being vulnerable to what they think may be their failures, insecurities, dilemmas . . . all those felt difficulties. I get to go into their worlds in a profound way. These are the conversations where their relationships with kids start becoming revealed, where their hearts begin to peek out from behind the safety of "teacher speak."

I have seen inquiry transform the lives of so many teachers with whom I work. It has also transformed my own life as a teacher, in a way that—one day—I hope to be able to fully articulate. Thanks for letting me practice here on the computer screen.

—Darby

PASSION PROFILES ACTIVITY

---

pas·sion (p²sh" . . . n) *n.* **1.** A powerful emotion, such as love, joy, hatred, or anger. **2.a.** Ardent love. **3.a.** Boundless enthusiasm . . .

Read the passion profiles and identify the passion that most accurately describes who you are as an educator. If several fit (this will be true for many of you), choose the one that affects you the most, or the one that seems most significant as you reflect on your practice over time. [five minutes]

Without using the number of the passion profile, ask your colleagues questions and find the people who chose the same profile you did. [five minutes]

Directions for Small Groups:

1. Choose a facilitator/timer and a recorder/reporter.

2. Check to see if you all really share that passion. Then, talk about your school experiences together. What is it like to have this passion—to be this kind of educator? Each person in the group should have an opportunity to talk, uninterrupted, for two minutes. [ten minutes]

3. Next, each person in the group privately identifies an actual student, by name, who has been affected by the group's profile. Write in your journal: [five minutes]
   - What have I done with this student?
   - What's worked? What hasn't?
   - What else could I do?
   - What questions does this raise for me?

4. Talk as a group about the questions that teachers who share this passion are likely to have about their practice. List as many of these questions as you can. [fifteen minutes]

   The recorder/reporter should write on the newsprint, and should be ready to report out succinctly to the large group. Be sure to put your passion profile number at the top of the newsprint page.

5. Whole group debrief (after hearing from each passion profile group): [fifteen minutes]
   - What strikes you as you listen to the passions of these educators? Listen for the silences. Where are they, and what do you make of them?
   - Which of the questions generated intrigues you the most? Why? How might you go about exploring this question with colleagues? What would you do first?

PASSION PROFILES

Passion 1: The Child

You became a teacher primarily because you wanted to make a difference in the life of a child. Perhaps you were one of those whose life was changed by a committed, caring teacher and you decided to become a teacher so that you could do that for other children. You are always curious about particular students whose work and/or behavior just doesn't seem to be in sync with the rest of the students in your class. You often wonder about how peer interactions seem to affect a student's likelihood to complete assignments, or what enabled one of your English language learning students to make such remarkable progress seemingly overnight, or how to motivate a particular student to get into the habit of writing. You believe that understanding the unique qualities that each student brings to your class is the key to unlocking all their full potential as learners.

Passion 2: The Curriculum

You are one of those teachers who are always "tinkering" with the curriculum to enrich the learning opportunities for your students. You have a thorough understanding of your content area. You attend conferences and subscribe to journals that help you to stay up on current trends affecting the curriculum that you teach. Although you are often dissatisfied with "what is" with respect to the prescribed curriculum in your school or district, you are almost always sure that you could do it better than the frameworks. You are always critiquing the existing curriculum and finding ways to make it better for the kids you teach—especially when you have a strong hunch that "there is a better way to do this."

Passion 3: Content Knowledge

You are at your best in the classroom when you have a thorough understanding of the content and/or topic you are teaching. Having to teach something you don't know much about makes you uncomfortable and always motivates you to hone up this area of your teaching knowledge base. You realize that what you know about what you are teaching will influence how you get it across to your students in a developmentally appropriate way. You spend a considerable amount of your personal time—both during the school year and in the summer—looking for books, material, workshops, and courses you can take that will strengthen your content knowledge.

Passion 4: Teaching Strategies

You are motivated most as a teacher by a desire to improve on and experiment with teaching strategies and techniques. You have experienced and understand the value of particular strategies to engage students in powerful learning and want to get really good at this stuff.

Although you have become really comfortable with using cooperative learning with your students, there are many other strategies and techniques that interest you and that you want to incorporate into your teaching repertoire.

Passion 5: The Relationship Between Beliefs and Professional Practice

You sense a disconnect between what you believe and what actually happens in your classroom and/or school. For example, you believe that a major purpose of schools is to produce citizens capable of contributing to and sustaining a democratic society; however, students in your class seldom get an opportunity to discuss controversial issues because you fear that the students you teach may not be ready and/or capable of this and you are concerned about losing control of the class.

Passion 6: The Intersection Between Your Personal and Professional Identities

You came into teaching from a previous career and often sense that your previous identity may be in conflict with your new identity as an educator. You feel ineffective and frustrated when your students or colleagues don't approach a particular task that is second nature to you because of your previous identity—e.g., writer, actor, artist, researcher—in the same way that you do. What keeps you up at night is how to use the knowledge, skills, and experiences you bring from your previous life to make powerful teaching and learning happen in your classroom and/or school.

Passion 7: Advocating Equity and Social Justice

You became an educator to change the world—to help create a more just, equitable, democratic, and peaceful planet. You are constantly thinking of ways to integrate issues of race, class, disability, power, and the like into your teaching; however, your global concerns for equity and social justice sometimes get in the way of your effectiveness as an educator—like the backlash that resulted from the time you showed *Schindler's List* to your sixth grade class. You know there are more developmentally appropriate ways to infuse difficult and complex issues into your teaching and want to learn more about how to do this with your students.

Passion 8: Context Matters

What keeps you up at night is how to keep students focused on learning despite the many disruptions that go on in your classroom/building on a daily basis. It seems that the school context conspires against everything that you know about teaching and learning—adults who don't model the behaviors they want to see reflected in the students, policies that are in conflict with the school's mission, and above all a high-stakes testing environment that tends to restrain the kind of teaching and learning that you know really works for the students you teach.

4

Helping PLC Members Develop an Action Research Plan

An elderly man had lived his entire life in the same small town. Approaching his sixtieth birthday, he decided to venture out of his small town to explore the ways people lived in other parts of the world. Excited by the prospect of his journey, he filled his car up with gas, and began driving. He had some general notions of where he might head, but did not bother to chart a course for his travels or bring a road map. Before long, he found himself wandering aimlessly from road to road, town to town, and he had lost sight of why he began this trip in the first place. He returned to the comfort of his home without the enrichment or insights that travel can bring.

Like the elderly gentleman in the vignette that opened this chapter, in the absence of a well-developed plan for inquiry, teacher-researchers risk making little or no progress in their work, getting lost, and even returning to the comfort of the ways their teaching has always been done without the benefits and insights that inquiry can bring. Hence, one critical component of coaching inquiry within your PLC is creating an opportunity for teachers to construct a road map and chart the course for their inquiry journeys. The purpose of this chapter is to help you create that opportunity.

Once the process of action research is ignited with the birth of a wondering, the next step in the coaching process is to support members of your PLC in the development of their road map in the form of an *inquiry brief*, defined by Hubbard and Power (1999) as "a detailed outline completed before the research study begins" (p. 47). In general, a research brief may cover such aspects as the purpose of your study, your wonderings, how you will collect data, how you will analyze data, and a timeline for your study (Dana & Yendol-Silva, 2003). An example of an inquiry brief, completed by high school English teacher, Tom Beyer (2007), is found in Figure 4.1.

Through the process of developing a brief, teacher-inquirers commit their energies to one idea. The process also helps members gain insights into their wondering(s) and the "doability" of action research becomes apparent. Through the development of an inquiry brief, your PLC membership develops a sense of direction and knows where to go next.

Figure 4.1 Inquiry Brief Example

Sample Inquiry Brief

Tom Beyer

Purpose

I love to read. I grew up with my parents reading to me at night and any other time I could persuade them to pick up a book. My love of literature and reading continued to grow throughout grade school and into high school. In college, it tapered off due to my course load, but I still found time to pick up a good book and get carried away to another world. Something has troubled me lately, and I want to gather some concrete data to either confirm my suspicions—or hopefully, prove them wrong. The rapid advances in technology have provided an increasing number of options available for students to spend their free time. As I thought about the things I had available to entertain me when I was growing up, I realized that the generation that is going through high school now has many more options than I had twelve years ago. When I was a senior, we still had regular pep rallies and a Friday night football game or basketball game was a major event where the community came together and supported the team—in other words: it was a priority. Similarly, if you weren't going to a movie, shopping, or working: reading a good book was a viable option. The internet hadn't taken a firm hold yet—libraries still served as the primary location for research (vice the family computer in the living room or a student's laptop nowadays). Hence, I want to know what the reading habits are of the high school seniors that I teach—is their interest in reading tapering off?

Questions

What are the reading habits of my high school seniors?

Method

I teach approximately 100 seniors over my four periods of twelfth grade English. I plan to begin by interviewing one or two students from each of my different classes: Advanced Placement, Honors, and English IV. Based on what I learn in the interviews, I will develop a survey to give out to all of my students and then I will analyze the results. I plan to conduct multiple sessions in which the students read silently for a sustained amount of time, while I observe them. Sessions will be announced and I will take field notes on such areas as: what they are reading, how long it takes them to settle in, and did they bring something to read. I plan on holding a few open forums with each group to discuss their reading habits and interview a small sample of students to go beyond the survey questions. For the interviews, I will pick students from different ability groups and students who are achieving different grades and interview them as a small group and individually.

Data Collection

- Observation/field notes of reading sessions, interviews, and open forums
- Survey results
- Any additional reflections from students
- Discussions with peers about this guided inquiry

Calendar

January 2007

- Interview a few students from each class
- Develop and administer survey and review answers
- Look for patterns and trends in responses
- Conduct silent sustained reading (SSR) sessions

February 2007

- Conduct SSR sessions
- Conduct open forums
- Continue to collect data

March 2007

- Conduct small group and individual interviews
- Begin data analysis

April 2007

- Complete data analysis
- Write paper summarizing results to share with my peers
- Present my work at the inquiry showcase

FACILITATING THE DEVELOPMENT OF AN INQUIRY BRIEF: THE INQUIRY-PLANNING MEETING

If members of your PLC have elected to explore a single wondering or a series of related wonderings together, the process of developing an inquiry brief can be accomplished by dedicating one PLC meeting to this purpose. The coach may begin this meeting by stating and posting the agreed-upon wondering, and facilitating a meeting that will result in devising a plan to systematically explore that wondering. Important components of this plan will include addressing the following questions: "How will we collect data to gain insights into this question?" "How will we analyze this data?" "When will we collect the data?" "Who will collect the data?" And, "How will we share the results of our work?" A peek into a meeting led by PLC Coach Kevin helps to illustrate this process.

Kevin's PLC had been meeting since just before school opened in August. During the group's early meetings, members engaged in a series of conversations about their struggling students' needs and a series of readings related to engaged instruction. One of the topics that generated much attention from these early group discussions was the role that culturally responsive teaching might play in helping the teachers reach their struggling students. The group had learned that culturally responsive teaching uses the cultural knowledge, prior experiences, and performance styles of diverse students to make learning more appropriate and effective by teaching to and through the strengths of these students (Gay, 2000). Additionally, the group had come to recognize culturally responsive teaching as multidimensional, including elements of: curriculum content, learning context, classroom climate, student-teacher relationships, instructional techniques, and performance assessments.

As a result of this shared learning and identification of a shared goal, the group gave birth to the following wonderings: *How do we create more culturally responsive teaching in our classrooms? What happens to student learning when we create more culturally responsive teaching?* The group believed that this work connected to a larger context including the school's improvement plan, the district's initiative, and the community's needs.

In mid-October the group met to begin developing its inquiry plan. The meeting began with ten minutes devoted to a protocol called "Connections" designed to help learning community members build a bridge from where they are or have been (e.g., mentally, physically) to where they will be going and what they will be doing in this PLC meeting (see the NSRF Web site for additional instructions on this protocol—http://www.harmonyschool.org/nsrf/protocol/index.html).

Once "Connections" was completed, Kevin began, "We left our last PLC meeting with two questions that we agreed to explore together this year." Kevin pointed to the chart paper he had hung up prior to the start of the meeting that read, "How do we create more culturally responsive teaching in our classrooms? What happens to student learning when we create more culturally responsive teaching?" He knew it would be important to have that question front and center during each of their meetings in order to keep the group's eye on the goal.

He continued, "I think that at today's meeting, it might be beneficial for us to develop a plan for how our inquiry will proceed, but first I need to confirm that we are all comfortable with the decision to pursue this question, and committed to engaging in action research in order to pursue it. The floor is open for thoughts and comments for five minutes."

PLC membership dialogue ensued, reaffirming the membership's commitment toward culturally responsive practices and the action research process.

At the end of five minutes, Kevin spoke, "I hear we all share a passion and commitment to devote our PLC work to the exploration of this question, so let's begin by discussing how we could collect data to explore this question. Let's brainstorm a list of the information we would need to help us answer this question, and then match up data collection strategies that would help us generate this information. This is a time to be open to all possibilities and not limit our brainstorming in any way, so let's begin."

Kevin drew a two-column chart on the whiteboard that he filled in as PLC members generated ideas. The group began by generating a list of the types of information that they believed would help them better understand their students and their students' culture, and Kevin listed this information in the left-hand column (see Figure 4.2).

When no new ideas were forthcoming from PLC group members, Kevin stood and admired the chart they had created together. They had created a lengthy list of areas they knew they needed more knowledge about in order to teach these struggling students. Next, Kevin brainstormed with the group the kinds of data that would help members get the information they deemed potentially useful. In the right-hand column of the chart, Kevin scripted their ideas. Figure 4.2 represents the chart that was generated by the group.

Although the group seemed pleased with the list, some members looked overwhelmed at the amount of data that was at hand. As a result, Kevin proceeded to ask the group to carefully evaluate the chart and the data suggestions as he posed the following questions:

- What data collection strategies that appeared on our list surprised you?
- What data collection strategies would be great sources of data, but impractical to obtain?
- What sources of data do you think would be most valuable and why?
- What structures need to be in place to support this data collection effort?

Through discussion of these questions, the group committed to collecting and analyzing a variety of data sources to gain insights into the question. For example, at the beginning of their work together, the group members decided to distribute a survey to both parents and students to better

Figure 4.2   Data Collection Exercise

Shared Inquiry Questions:
How do we create more culturally responsive teaching in our classrooms?
What happens to student learning when we create more culturally
responsive teaching?

Information That Would Help Us Answer Our Question	Data Collection Strategies That Would Generate This Information
Find out more about the neighborhoods our students live in.	Field notes
Find out what parents expect from the school community.	Survey Home visits
Find out how our students are performing in each academic area and subarea.	Assessment data
Find out what goals students set for themselves.	Student interviews/surveys
Find out what management patterns are familiar to students; find out what teachers expect from their students and how they encourage students to meet expectations and recognize their accomplishments.	Focus groups with teachers Classroom observations
Get to know students' learning style preferences.	Survey
Utilize content and resources that connect to students' backgrounds.	A search for books, articles, and Web resources Journaling about new strategies that might benefit your students and why
Develop a variety of learning activities that are engaging and reflective of students' backgrounds (cooperative learning, literature circles, community projects).	A search for books, articles, and Web resources Journaling about new strategies that might benefit your students and why
Find out how students respond (both learning and engagement) to various teaching strategies.	Student work analysis Field notes Student feedback sheets Journaling about changes you are seeing in your teaching and with your students

understand their own goals as well as expectations they had of the school. During the bulk of the year, the group members also believed that saving student work samples, tracking student growth on assessments, as well as notes from peer observations would help them make sense of their ability to transfer new ideas about culturally responsive teaching to the classroom. All of the members also committed to keeping a journal that included field notes as well as personal reflections on their teaching. Finally, they decided that by asking students to complete feedback sheets after engaging in culturally relevant teaching, they would be able to include student voices in the findings.

Kevin continued, "Okay, great, we have a plan for collecting data. Now, we need to establish when and how we are going to do this plan. Our PLC meetings are the first Wednesday of every month. How about if I list our monthly meeting dates on the board and we can use that to set goals for when this data is collected, not to mention which of us will be involved in collecting it, when we'll do some analysis, and then we'll share what we learned with others. Clearly, some data we will all be collecting, but some data (like the survey data), we should divide and conquer." Through discussion, the timeline represented in Figure 4.3 emerged.

As shown, this plan integrated the inquiry process as well as many of the protocols for looking at student work, resolving dilemmas, and generating lesson plans that are offered by the NSRF as tools for deepening teaching practice. Additionally, the plan required the learning community members to do data collection outside of the learning community meeting times, and the principal of the school could allocate this important time for the teachers and Kevin to engage in the professional work associated with the inquiry.

Once the shared question had been formed, the data collection plan generated, and the timeline created, Kevin asked the group to evaluate its work so far using a set of prompts that help teacher-researchers maintain the integrity of their work. These were thoughts that Kevin regularly kept in the back of his mind as he coached and now he would make those questions explicit to his group: (1) Have we established a connection between the inquiry question and all other components of the inquiry plan (data collection, data analysis, timeline)? (2) Are we using multiple forms of data? (3) Is our plan doable? And (4) Can we make our timeline for implementing the inquiry plan work?

As coach, Kevin volunteered to type up the plan, and ended the PLC meeting with a reminder, "We have engaged in some hard work today to develop a plan for our inquiry. I'll type up our work and e-mail it to everyone before our next meeting. I will also be keeping a notebook of the artifacts we generate from our inquiry work, but we will each need to keep our own inquiry notebook as well. Just as I will document our collective work, you must each document your individual work toward making sense of how culturally responsive teaching is working for you and your students.

"I also want us all to keep in mind, however, that even though we commit a plan to paper, it's okay for us to deviate from our plan as our inquiry unfolds. We may discover something along the way in our data that leads us in a new direction. We can help each other remain open to shifts in our inquiry along the way by periodically returning to this plan and suggesting modifications. We need to remember that the plan we constructed today is important to provide direction, but it isn't set in stone! Let's spend our final five minutes writing a reflection on today's meeting." PLC group

Figure 4.3 Timeline for Inquiry

How do we create more culturally responsive teaching in our classrooms? What happens to student learning when we create more culturally responsive teaching?

Month	Before Meeting	During Meeting
September	• Read articles on culturally responsive teaching (all members) • Review own student assessment data	• Connections • Text-based discussion on articles • Establish groups' shared goals and inquiry questions • Reflection
October	• Develop, distribute, and collect parent and student surveys (Jane, Mark, and Beth) • Collect and review baseline assessment data (each classroom teacher) • Visit neighborhoods (entire PLC; invite pastor)	• Connections • Analyze parent and student surveys using the chalk talk protocol • Engage in a text-based discussion of culturally responsive teaching strategies • Reflection
November	• Student interviews (each teacher completes three interviews) • Peer observation (each teacher observes one other group member) • Collect student work as teacher implements culturally responsive teaching strategies (each teacher) • Take field notes as teacher implements culturally responsive teaching strategies (each teacher)	• Connections • Tuning protocols or dilemma protocols focused on teachers sharing their efforts to engage in culturally responsive teaching strategies (three presenters; four groups) • Analyze student interviews • Reflection
December	• Read article about culturally responsive teaching strategies (each teacher) • Peer observations (each teacher observes one other group member) • Collect student work • Take field notes as teacher implements culturally responsive teaching strategies (each teacher) • Review student assessment data (each teacher)	• Connections • Engage in a text-base discussion of culturally responsive teaching strategies • Tuning protocols or dilemma protocols focused on teachers sharing their efforts to engage in culturally responsive teaching strategies (three presenters; four groups) • Reflection
January	• Collect student work • Peer observations (each teacher observes one other group member) • Take field notes as teacher implements culturally responsive teaching strategies (each teacher)	• Connections • Use protocols to analyze student work • Use consultancy to explore dilemmas you are having with your students • Reflection

Month	Before Meeting	During Meeting
February	• Collect student work • Peer observations (each teacher observes one other group member) • Take field notes as teacher implements culturally responsive teaching strategies (each teacher)	• Connections • Use protocols to analyze student work • Use consultancy to explore dilemmas you are having with your students • Reflection
March	• Collect student work samples • Take field notes as teacher implements culturally responsive teaching strategies (each teacher) • Review student assessment data (each teacher) • Meet with Kevin (each teacher met with Kevin or another trained coach in the school to closely examine the individual data that he or she had collected)	• Connections • Use protocols to analyze student work • Use consultancy to explore dilemmas you are having with your students • Reflection
April	• Repeat survey (Jennifer, Mike, Angi) • Repeat subset of student interviews • Gather all data • Engage in preliminary analysis by reading through own data	• Connections • Analyze survey data • Analyze data across learning community meetings to generate overarching findings from the year's inquiry work • Reflection
May	• Develop presentation	• Provide an overview of results to principal • Share at faculty meeting and with district office • Reflection

members took out a piece of paper, and jotted down their feelings and thoughts about the ways their inquiry-planning meeting had transpired.

● ● ●

When developing a group inquiry brief, as in the case of Kevin described above, a number of individuals are contributing to the plan as it emerges. The end result of the PLC inquiry-planning meeting is the brief itself. Because it is a group process, the brief is both constructed and fine-tuned at the same time. Kevin was always keeping in mind the key components that make inquiry work and would prompt his group to consider these ideas along the way. However, if you are coaching a PLC where members are each exploring different questions, it is often helpful for each individual to come to the inquiry-planning meeting with an inquiry brief already developed, and enough copies for each member of the group. Hence, rather than the inquiry-planning meeting *ending* with one brief that is both fine-tuned and constructed at the same time by the entire group, the inquiry-planning meeting *begins* with an individual PLC member presenting his or her already developed brief and receiving feedback from PLC group members to fine-tune the plan. Subsequently, each member of the PLC takes a turn presenting and receiving feedback on his or her individual brief. When all members of the PLC have received feedback, the meeting ends with the writing of reflective statements on the brief-tuning experience.

We have found that it is helpful to use a protocol to provide structure to inquiry-planning meetings focused on the individual presenting his or her brief and to be sure everyone in the group gets equal time for feedback and tuning. Figure 4.4 provides an example of a protocol we developed for this purpose. If your PLC has more than five members, we suggest you break into groups of three or four to engage with this protocol.

Sometimes, in addition to or in lieu of participating in an inquiry-planning meeting for individuals to cycle through sharing their own briefs and providing feedback on the briefs of others, a teacher-inquirer may seek out help from his or her coach, asking the coach to review his or her brief and provide personal feedback. Other times a teacher-inquirer may "try out" ideas on the inquiry coach as he or she writes the inquiry brief.

Similar to the wondering litmus test in Chapter 3, in the next section, we raise a series of questions facilitators can pose to themselves when they read a brief or hear an inquirer discuss a plan for study. By considering these questions, a coach can engage in dialogue with the inquirer to tune the plan until wondering, data collection, data analysis, and timeline for implementation of the inquiry are clearly articulated and all in alignment with one another. The evolution of an inquiry plan based on a coach's consideration of these questions is illustrated through the work of one teacher-inquirer Nancy coached—Debbi Hubbell.

THE INQUIRY BRIEF LITMUS TEST

Is there correlation between the inquiry question and all other components of the inquiry plan (e.g., data collection, data analysis, timeline)?

Is the teacher-researcher using multiple forms of data?

Has the teacher-researcher already (or does the teacher-researcher plan to) connect his or her work to a larger context (e.g., a school's improvement plan, a district initiative, research already completed on the topic)?

Is the design of the study experimental?

Is the inquiry plan doable?

Does the inquirer have a timeline for implementing the inquiry plan?

Figure 4.4 Inquiry Brief Tuning Protocol

**Inquiry Brief Discussion Protocol:
Six Steps to a Fine-Tuned Plan for Inquiry**

Suggested Group Size: 3–4
Suggested Time Frame: 15–20 MINUTES PER GROUP MEMBER

1. Select a timekeeper.

2. Presenter hands out a hard copy of the inquiry brief to each member of the group.

3. Group members *silently* read the inquiry brief, making notes of issues/questions they might like to raise in discussion with presenter [four minutes]. As group members read the brief, presenter engages in a writing activity to complete the following sentences:
   Something I would like help with on my inquiry brief is . . .

   One thing this group needs to know about me or my proposed inquiry to better prepare them to assist me is . . .

4. At the end of four minutes (or when it is clear that every member of the group has completed reading and taking notes on the inquiry brief, and the presenter has finished his or her response to the writing activity), the timekeeper invites the presenter to read his or her sentence completion activity out-loud [no more than one minute].

5. Participants talk to each other as if the presenter was not in the room, while the presenter remains silent and takes notes [approximately ten minutes]. Participants focus on *each* of the following:
   - Provide "warm feedback" on the inquiry brief. This is feedback that is positive in nature and identifies areas of strength. [one to two minutes]
   - Address the area the presenter would like help on and discuss the following questions [eight to ten minutes]:
     A. What match seems to exist (or not exist) between the proposed data collection plan and inquiry question?
     B. Are there additional types of data that would give the participant insights into his or her question?
     C. Rate the doability of this plan for inquiry. In what ways is the participant's plan meshed with the everyday work of a teacher?
     D. In what ways does the participant's proposed timeline for study align with each step in the action research process?
     E. What possible disconnects and problems do you see?

6. Timekeeper asks presenter to summarize the key points made during discussion that he or she wishes to consider in refining the plan for inquiry. [one minute]

SOURCE: Developed by Nancy Fichtman Dana and Diane Yendol-Hoppey.

With more than a decade of elementary teaching experience behind her, Debbi was approached by her principal and asked if she wished to participate in a professional development opportunity that would last the entire school year—learning about and engaging in action research. After Debbi had gone through the process, she would then help to teach others at their school about action research as staff development, as well as support her colleagues in their own action research endeavors in subsequent school years. Debbi was excited about the opportunity, and eagerly attended the first full-day meeting, where she was provided with an overview of the entire action research process through the presentations of teachers who had previously engaged in inquiry. In addition, Debbi was provided with a book, *The Reflective Educator's Guide to Classroom Research* (Dana & Yendol-Silva, 2003) that would guide her through each component of the action research process step by step.

Debbi was grouped with four other teachers from surrounding districts, along with Nancy, her inquiry coach. Nancy explained that they'd be meeting once a month, forming a PLC to support each other in their own inquiry endeavors. They engaged in a series of activities that helped them get to know each other, to set ground rules for the ways the group would function as they met several times that school year, and to explore possible topics and wonderings associated with those topics to frame their first inquiries.

In one of these activities, Debbi articulated that she was passionate about reading, and in particular, fluency. Debbi's school had been one of thirteen schools to pilot a statewide program called the Florida Reading Initiative. In addition, her school had set a goal as part of its annual school improvement planning process to raise the fluency levels of the lowest-achieving students in order to increase their performance on the reading portion of their state's standardized test—FCAT (Florida Comprehensive Assessment Test). Finally, Debbi was a voracious reader and had been studying the literature on reading fluency. She knew the research indicated that a correlation exists between fluency and comprehension. Perhaps a focus on fluency would help her struggling readers perform better on FCAT.

Debbi left the meeting with a list of brainstormed potential wonderings she had related to the fluency development of her students, and the assignment to read about the finer points of developing a wondering and inquiry brief in her book. In addition, Debbi was to prepare an inquiry brief for their next meeting in three weeks, bringing enough copies for all members of her group.

As Debbi began to work on her brief, she called her coach to "try out" some of her ideas. Nancy and Debbi decided to meet on Wednesday afternoon to discuss her emerging plan for research. After a few minutes of casual conversation, Debbi got to the point of their meeting:

"Well, it's great to see you again, and thanks for agreeing to meet with me to help me work on my brief. I'm not sure how to word my wondering, but what I want to investigate is fluency with my fourth graders. Research shows that repeated readings improve fluency. I'd like to see if there is a difference in fluency gains between using a commercial reading program we have purchased in our district called Great Leaps and repeated readings of plays with my students. I have a book of plays that are "fractured fairy tales," that seem as if they would be very motivational for fourth grade learners. They're basically humorous takes on traditional fairy tales. I think they have the potential to boost the fluency scores of my lowest readers on the assessment my district uses to track fluency development—DIBELS. If you're not familiar with DIBELS, it stands for Dynamic Indicators of Basic Early Literacy Skills, a set of standardized, individually administered measures of literacy development. They are designed to be short (one minute) fluency measures used to regularly monitor the development of prereading and early reading skills. So, I'm thinking I could divide my lowest performing students into two different reading groups—I can use the Great Leaps program with one group and the fractured fairy tales with the other group and then compare their DIBELS scores to see which group had higher gains."

Nancy paused and thought for a minute. As she had been listening to Debbi articulate plans for her inquiry, a few things ran through her head. First, she was not surprised that Debbi's initial study design emulated the design of a traditional experimental study. In her experience coaching, she found that first-time action researchers were often drawn to experimental designs in the early stages of developing a plan for their research. Nancy attributed this inclination toward experimental studies to all the baggage the word *research* carried with it. When teachers first hear the word *research*, they often conjure images of formulating a hypothesis and setting up comparison groups—one to receive a "treatment," and one to remain "the control."

In her experience, Nancy also knew that rarely does it make sense for an action research study to take this form, as teacher action research is generally about capturing the natural actions that occur in the busy, real world of the classroom. In addition, by and large, a single teacher's classroom usually is not a ripe place to design an experimental study since the sample size utilized in the study generally would not be adequate to indicate any statistical differences, and any one treatment variable (such as the reading of fractured fairy tales) would almost be impossible to isolate from intervening variables such as phonics and intonation. Finally, one would need to question the ethics of providing a potentially beneficial "treatment" to some children within a classroom but not to all.

Nancy began her response with some warm feedback, "I think you sound like you've got a *fantastic* focus for your inquiry! Reading fluency is definitely an area that many teachers and whole schools are looking at much more closely these days, especially based on research that indicates a relationship between fluency and comprehension. It's wonderful that your passion relates closely to a schoolwide goal as well as the literature on reading. I also think it makes a good deal of sense to focus on implementing a teaching strategy that you think would be motivational and enjoyable for children—the reading of fractured fairy-tale plays.

"One thing you might want to consider a bit more is the way you are thinking about your inquiry as a comparison between two different programs and two groups of children. I have found in my work with teachers over the years that often, initially, we tend to always think of research or inquiry in terms of comparison, sort of like an experimental study. In reality, it's really hard to control variables between two different groups or treatments—for example, in your case, the children who would work with the Great Leaps program and the children who will do the fractured fairy tales. You might want to simplify. Let me ask you a question, if you weren't about to embark on an action research project, would you, in the natural ways that you think about teaching, assign your struggling readers to two different groups and teach them in two different ways?"

Debbi thought for a moment and responded, "No, I don't think I would. If I wasn't trying to design a plan for my inquiry, I think I would just try the use of fractured fairy tales with all of my struggling readers, and see what kinds of results I would get."

"Okay then," Nancy responded. "If you wouldn't assign kids to two differently taught groups as a natural part of your teaching, then you might want to rethink your initial plan for inquiry. Would it work for you if you developed a plan to try fractured fairy tales with all of your struggling readers, and look closely at the ways the introduction of this new strategy plays out in the classroom? In essence, rather than looking at cause and effect, you would be looking at the general relationship that develops between the reading of fractured fairy tales and fluency development in struggling fourth grade learners over time."

"I like that," Debbi shared. "It feels more comfortable to me. And I think that I could still use DIBELS data as an indicator of fluency growth for data."

"Yes, that definitely would be one data source that would give insights into your wondering. Are there any others?"

"Hmmm. I'm not sure. I guess I'm still caught up in traditional notions of research and I think in terms of data being numbers, but I suppose I could also collect any student work that was generated in relationship to the fractured fairy-tale play readings, and see if I notice any changes over time. And I've read that many teacher-researchers keep a journal. I guess I could write down things I'm noticing after each fractured fairy-tale reading that I might otherwise forget if I didn't record it in some way."

Nancy smiled, "Now you're cooking! One of the most wonderful aspects of the teacher inquiry process is that it honors all of the great complexities inherent in teaching. Through teacher research, we can systematically tease apart some of that great complexity and develop a rich picture of what is occurring in the classroom in relationship to a wondering. Any one data source, whether it be student performance on a test or an assessment, student work, teacher anecdotal notes, a teacher-researcher's journal, survey responses, interviews, field notes, photographs, lesson plans, or any other documents produced as a result of teaching, only provides one piece of the picture. Rich teacher research relies on more than one source of data to create a more complete picture of what is occurring in relationship to the wondering posed. Using multiple sources of data and data collection strategies can enhance your inquiry as you gain differing perspectives from differing strategies.

"In addition, by employing multiple strategies, you can build a strong case for your findings by pointing out the ways different data sources all led you to the same conclusions, a process research methodologists refer to as triangulation" (Cresswell, 2002; Patton, 2000). "Finally, by employing multiple data sources you enhance your opportunities for learning when different data sources lead to discrepancies. It is often through posturing explanations for these discrepancies that the most powerful learning of teacher inquiry occurs, and that new wonderings for subsequent inquiries are generated."

Debbi carefully considered Nancy's comments about relying on more than one source of data and queried, "Are there other data collection strategies that you think I might use that could be insightful to my study?"

Nancy replied, "Well I heard you say that you believe the reading of fractured fairy tales might be motivational for your learners. I always think it's a good idea in an inquiry such as yours to collect some sort of data to give you insights into the perceptions your learners held of the new strategy you employed. You might interview some students after you are done with your fractured fairy tale unit, or even collect some data by having them reflect in writing on the fractured fairy-tale experience. In fourth grade, you might have them compose "Dear Mrs. Hubbell" letters where they tell you what they liked and disliked about reading fractured fairy tales."

"Wow, that's a great idea! I love the Dear Mrs. Hubbell letters because that actually kills two birds with one stone—my students have a meaningful writing assignment in which they have the opportunity to apply their writing skills, and I'll have another data source for my inquiry!"

"Sounds like a plan! As you think about using Dear Mrs. Hubbell letters as a data source, you might want to return to your wondering and tweak it a bit and/or develop one or two subwonderings that get at the relationship between fractured fairy-tale plays and student motivation to read. Now, have you thought through a timeline for your study? For this type of inquiry, you'll want to plan both the specifics of your implementation of the fractured fairy-tale plays as well as how you will collect and analyze the data as you go. When you bring your inquiry brief to our next PLC meeting, be sure to ask your group members to help you assess the doability of your plan. It's easy to go overboard and plan such large inquiries that they would be impossible to carry out. Keep this in mind as you develop your brief."

"I will. This discussion has been extremely helpful. I can't wait to get my inquiry started, and see what shape our other group member's inquiries are taking. I am very oriented toward considering data to be only things like scores on assessments such as DIBELS and standardized test scores, so I'm new to this type of thinking. I look forward to seeing you at our next meeting."

"Me too! You are on a great track here! This will be a wonderful inquiry! I can hardly wait to see what you discover."

●●●

In the excerpt of Nancy and Debbi's dialogue above, Nancy runs through the inquiry brief litmus questions in her own mind to formulate some solid feedback on Debbi's emerging plan, as well as to formulate some questions for Debbi that help her consider some of the finer aspects of action research plan development. In many cases, it is not uncommon for some skepticism around the notion of research to surface, and a serious question to arise in the minds of PLC members during the inquiry plan development phase—"Is what we're doing *really* research?" To help coaches address this question, we end this chapter with one of our favorite explanations of the differences, but complementary nature, between traditional forms of research and teacher research, from the book, *Living the Questions: A Guide for Teacher Researchers* (1999) by Ruth Hubbard and Brenda Power.

Little r and Big R

When we first talk with teachers about the possibilities for research in their professional lives, they often recount negative experiences with research, and stereotypical views of what researchers do. As teacher Julie Ford explains:

When I think of research, I think of the Big R type and long hours in the library, notes that could fill a novel, and a bibliography several pages long. I think of tension and stress lurking in the shadows. Feeling as I do about Research, the thought of conducting it in my classroom didn't curl my toes. But as I read classroom-based research, I felt as though a door was beginning to open. My definition of research took a turn, and that familiar twinge of anxiety didn't come rushing forward.

Teachers are surprised and delighted to realize that research can focus on problems they are trying to solve in their own classrooms. At its best, teacher research is a natural extension of good teaching. Observing students closely, analyzing their needs, and adjusting the curriculum to fit the needs of all students have always been important skills demonstrated by fine teachers.

Teacher research involves collecting and analyzing data, as well as presenting it to others in a systematic way. But this research process involves the kinds of skills and classroom activities that already are a part of the classroom environment. As Glenda Bissex writes, a teacher-researcher is not a split personality, but a more complete teacher. While research is labor-intensive, so is good teaching. And the labor is similar for teachers, because the end goal is the same—to create the best possible learning environment for students ...

(The research agenda) of most teachers are a kind of "dance" between teachers, students, and learning. Teacher-researchers rarely seek to initiate and carry out studies that have large-scale implications for education policy. Unlike large-scale education research, teacher research has a primary purpose of helping the teacher-researcher understand her students and improve her practice in specific, concrete ways. Teacher research studies can and do lead to large-scale education change. But for most teacher-researchers, the significance of the study is in how it informs and changes her own teaching ...

Lawrence Stenhouse noted that the difference between the teacher-researcher and the large-scale education researcher is like the difference between a farmer with a huge agricultural business to maintain and the "careful gardener" tending a backyard plot:

> In agriculture the equation of invested input against gross yield is all: it does not matter if individual plants fail to thrive or die so long as the cost of saving them is greater than the cost of losing them. ... This does not apply to the careful gardener whose labour is not costed, but a labour of love. He wants each of his plants to thrive, and he can treat each one individually. Indeed he can grow a hundred different plants in his garden and differentiate his treatment of each, pruning his roses, but not his sweet peas. Gardening rather than agriculture is the analogy for education. (Rudduck & Hopkins 1985, p. 26)

This view of the teacher-researcher as a "careful gardener" is the image we hold in our minds of the ideal teacher-researcher—not a scientist in a lab coat, staring down at a "research subject" (a kid!), but a human being in the midst of teaching, carefully weighing the value of different ways of teaching and learning (pp. 3–4).

As your PLC members develop and tune their inquiry plans, remind them that they are not trying to emulate the scientist in a lab coat, but the careful gardener.

5

Helping
PLC Members
Analyze Data

In relationship to their work, a woman, her husband, and two young children had the opportunity to travel through all of Australia for two full months. On their return to the United States, the woman rushed to develop the ten rolls of film she had shot throughout their travels. When the film was developed three days later, she whisked the almost 400 pictures out of the store and went straight to her parents' house. One by one, they went through each of the pictures in the order they were taken from the envelopes. After sitting at the kitchen table for two hours, they still had three envelopes yet to open and view. The woman sensed the fatigue felt by her parents, and her heart grew heavy as she realized that laboring through every single picture did not convey to others the magnificence of their trip. The pictures were in no meaningful order, some were blurry, and in some cases, there were way too many photographs of the same things.

Returning home, her husband eagerly greeted her at the door and queried, "Well, how did the pictures come out?" The woman sighed as she explained that the number of pictures was overwhelming her, and while many came out great, there were some that were out of focus, and during some parts of their trip, they must had been too camera happy—there were way too many shots that were similar. The woman feared that the pictures, that potentially held so much meaning for their family and their children's memories, would become a meaningless pile placed in a box and stored away in the attic. She imagined her young children all grown up, telling others that at one point in their lives, they had lived eight weeks in Australia, but they were so young, they hardly remembered a thing.

Disturbed by his wife's disappointment in the pictures, the man had an idea. He remembered that a new store had opened recently across town called Scrapbook Haven. He purchased a gift certificate and series of classes for his wife as a gift in hopes that this experience would help her capture their travels in a way that was meaningful and would have lasting impact on their two children.

The woman was grateful. At her first class, she learned that the best scrapbooks begin by sorting through pictures. "There's no need to use every single picture you brought to this class," the teacher said. "Why don't you look through every picture that was developed first, just to get a sense of what you have?" As the woman did so, she noticed she had some pictures from each stop on their itinerary. Some of the pictures were related to their work. Many of the pictures were of her two children.

Next, the teacher shared, "It is often helpful to group your pictures in different ways to decide how you want to proceed with the organization of your scrapbook. You might organize your scrapbook chronologically, or maybe by key events that took place during your trip, or perhaps even group pictures by individual child. Try sorting and resorting your pictures into piles that have some sort of meaning until you feel a sense of orderliness, commonality, and comfort with your assemblage.

The woman's first pass through her pictures was relatively easy. She sorted the pictures by stops on their travel itinerary, and then put the piles in chronological order. Next, she sorted each one of these piles into two subcategories—quality and nonquality photos. Quality photos were in focus, had good lighting, and were framed nicely by the photographer. Nonquality photos were out of focus, had some part of the subject being photographed cut out of the picture, or were photos she considered to be "bad" pictures of herself, her husband, or their children.

After looking at the piles, she noticed that three of them were of different stops on their itinerary, but were related as they were all pictures of families they had stayed with at different times during their trip. She combined these three piles together and placed a Post-it note on the pile that read, "Family Stays." She also noticed other piles that could be further divided up. For example, she had a pile of pictures she named "Caines, Australia" in the itinerary sort. Within this pile, however, there were multiple pictures of their time snorkeling over the Great Barrier Reef, multiple pictures of hiking in the Daintree Rainforest, and multiple pictures of swimming in the Coral Sea. She subdivided the "Caines" pile into these three subpiles, and in the process, realized that she had no photographs of their first stop in Caines—a visit to the Tjapukai Aboriginal Cultural Park, where her son learned to throw a boomerang. She would need to find the brochure from this park and add it to her Caines pictures once she returned home. In addition, there were a couple candid shots of their children at their hotel in Caines. She decided to remove these from the "Caines" subpiling and started a new pile called "Assorted Candids." She also found a few pictures of her daughter's fourth birthday party that must have been at the start of their first role of film they used in Australia. She placed these pictures aside and would not use them in the scrapbook.

After many iterations of the sorting process, the ways her scrapbook might take form began to become apparent to the woman. At this point, the teacher said, "It's time to create your first scrapbook page. Take one of your picture piles and arrange it on the page. Think about a statement you would like to write on this page that expresses the meaning this grouping of pictures holds for you. You also might want to add a title to your page. And remember, you don't have to use every single picture, and you might even use portions of a picture—it's okay to cut and paste."

The woman's class ended. She excitedly burst into her home and shared her hard work with her husband. Over time, she created a complete scrapbook of their travels. The final page contained a picture of her children back in their home in the states on the night they returned. The page was titled, "Home Sweet Home" and contained the following caption: "When we arrived home at 11:00 PM, jet lag had already set in as we were ready for breakfast, not bed. It took a few weeks to fully recover and reestablish our routines. It was good to be home, yet we will always fondly remember our days down under."

Upon its completion, the woman once again drove to her parent's house to share her new creation. As they turned each page of the scrapbook, short stories, humorous moments, and key experiences all seemed to jump out from the pages and fascinate her parents. The trip had been captured and conveyed to others in a way that never would have happened had the pictures stayed haphazardly thrown into a box labeled "Trip to Australia." The woman knew that the process of creating this book enabled her to better understand the enormous implications this eight-week excursion had for herself, her husband, and most importantly, her children. She knew that the scrapbook would serve as an important catalyst to trigger their memories as they grew into adulthood.

L ike the woman in the vignette that opened this chapter who lamented over the fact that she had developed nearly 400 pictures, but didn't know what to do with them so they would have meaning beyond just a big pile stored away in a box, teacher-researchers often find themselves overwhelmed when they get to the data analysis phase of their studies and face making sense of a huge pile of collected data. Hence, one critical component of coaching inquiry within your PLC is supporting the data analysis process. The purpose of this chapter is to provide some tools you may use to provide that support. These tools include a review of the data analysis process, suggestions for planning and running a PLC meeting devoted to data analysis, and a protocol developed specifically to help teacher-researchers dig deeper into their analyses.

DATA ANALYSIS FOR THE ACTION RESEARCHER: A REVIEW

The first tool we provide is a brief review of the data analysis process. First, it is important to note that data collection and analysis are often two processes that intertwine with each other throughout the action research cycle. This means that analysis isn't just something done at the end of an inquiry—teacher-researchers often move back and forth between collecting and analyzing data throughout an entire study.

One example of the flip-flop relationship between data collection and analysis comes from the work of twelfth grade English teacher and researcher Tom Beyer (2007), whose inquiry brief appears in Chapter 4. Tom wanted to better understand the reading habits of his students in order to more effectively differentiate the instruction for his Advanced Placement, Honors, and English IV classes. He began his work by pulling a student aside from each of these classes during homeroom, and posing a few questions about what and when each student read. Tom analyzed the notes he took on these interviews to determine questions he would utilize on a survey that would be given to all his students. Tom administered the survey, collecting the responses, and again returned to data analysis by tallying responses to survey questions and grouping narrative responses to the same questions together. The information he obtained in this portion of his study guided his observations of students during sustained silent reading time. He continued to collect data for a number of weeks after the initial interviews and surveys as he observed his students and took field notes. Analysis of his field notes led him to conduct further individual interviews with students who were selected based on what Tom observed. In addition, Tom held a whole-class focus group interview session toward the end of his study.

While Tom had engaged in some data analysis to give direction to his study as it proceeded from January through March, as he approached the end of the school year he placed all of his data—initial interviews, surveys, field notes, later interviews, and focus group notes—into one pile. It was now time to synthesize his learning by looking at his entire data set as a whole.

When teacher-inquirers get to this point in their inquiries, they often ponder: "Okay, I've collected all of this 'stuff,' and I have a whole crate full of data . . . *now* what do I do with it?" The findings and conclusions that teacher-researchers make at the end of a study do not materialize out of thin air—they come from careful scrutiny of their data sets as they proceed through a systematic process of making sense of what they learned.

Research methodologists have developed, described, and named a long list of systematic processes that facilitate data analysis. Two of the processes most frequently discussed in the social sciences are coding and memoing. We turn to Schwandt's (1997) *Qualitative Inquiry: A Dictionary of Terms* to provide brief, technical definitions of these concepts:

> **CODING**—To begin the process of analyzing the large volume of data generated in the form of transcripts, field notes, photographs, and the like, the qualitative inquirer engages in the activity of coding. Coding is a procedure that disaggregates that data, breaks it down into manageable segments, and identifies or names those segments. . . . Coding requires constantly comparing and contrasting various successive segments of the data and subsequently categorizing them. (p. 16)

> **MEMOING**—A procedure suggested by Barney Glaser (*Theoretical Sensitivity: Advances in the Methodology of Grounded Theory*, Sociology Press, 1978) for explaining or elaborating on the coded categories that the fieldworker develops in analyzing data. Memos are conceptual in intent, vary in length, and are primarily written to oneself. The content of memos can include commentary on the meaning of a coded category, explanation of a sense of pattern developing among categories, a *description* of some specific aspect of a setting or phenomenon, and so forth. Typically, the final analysis and

interpretation is based on integration and analysis of memos. (pp. 89–90)

While the data analysis work of a teacher-inquirer does draw from the field of social sciences and borrows the processes described by these scholars, it is easy to get bogged down in the *jargon* or technical language in the definitions above that are not a part of the daily language of teachers. Phrases such as *disaggregating data, coded categories, phenomenon,* and *final analysis and interpretation* may feel foreign to teaching practice and set up a roadblock to data analysis. To help teacher-researchers around this roadblock, we suggest that PLC coaches focus on describing the processes of data analysis named above with language, phrases and metaphors that are consonant with the life and work of a teacher. To aid in this process, in the remainder of this section, we review the data analysis process step-by-step using teacher-friendly language and phrases, as well as the scrapbooking story that opened this chapter as a metaphor for data analysis. We hope the language and metaphor we invoke to describe each step will be useful for you as you support the data analysis process of others.

Data Analysis Step One: Description

In the description phase, teacher-inquirers read and reread their entire data set, with no other objective than to get a *descriptive* sense of what they have collected. The goal of this first step of analysis is *to describe* the teacher-researcher's inquiry data. Like the scrapbook teacher in the opening vignette of this chapter who suggested, "Why don't you look through every picture that was developed first, just to get a sense of what you have?," PLC coaches can suggest that members of their PLC begin data analysis by reading through their entire data set. During their initial read of the data set, PLC coaches can help their group members by posing the following questions to consider as they read:

Why did you inquire?

What did you see as you inquired?

What was happening?

What are your initial insights into the data?

Data Analysis Step Two: Sense-Making

Next, teacher-inquirers begin the *sense-making* step by reading their data and asking questions such as, "What sorts of things are happening in my data?" "What do I notice?" "How might different pieces of my data fit together?" And, "What pieces of my data stand out from the rest?" Sometimes teachers take notes in the margins of their data, or write down their answers to these questions on a separate sheet of paper. Organizing data is one of the most creative parts of the sense-making process. Sometimes inquirers get stuck at this stage and need some prompts to help begin this sense-making process. Figure 5.1 offers some organizing units that coaches can offer to serve as prompts for helping teachers begin analysis.

Figure 5.1   Examples of Organizing Units

Examples of Organizing Units		
Chronology	Key events	Various settings
People	Processes	Behaviors
Issues	Relationships	Groups
Styles	Changes	Meanings
Practices	Strategies	Episodes
Encounters	Roles	Feelings

For example, teachers might look at their data and see if a story emerges that takes a *chronological* form. Teachers may notice that their data seems to be organizing itself around *key events.* Or, teachers may see some combination of organizing units that are helpful. The table in Figure 5.1 is by no means exhaustive, and teachers should let the organizing units emerge from their own data rather than forcing an external set of units.

Based on answers to the questions posed above and a teacher's emerging units of analysis, teacher-inquirers identify common themes or patterns, and begin a process of grouping or sorting data by theme or category, a process likened to the woman's initial sorting of her Australia pictures by "stops on the travel itinerary." One way to group data is to use a different color marker for each theme or pattern identified, and highlight all excerpts from the data that fit this theme or pattern. Another way of grouping data might be to physically cut it apart and place the data in different piles. If teachers do decide to cut the data apart, you might want to suggest they keep a complete set of data as a backup.

Just as our scrapbooker found some pictures from her daughter's fourth birthday, as teachers engage in this process, they will notice that not all of the data they collected will be highlighted or coded, or will fit with their developing patterns or themes. These diverging data excerpts should be acknowledge and explained if possible (e.g.,"Those pictures must have been at the start of our first role of film and don't really belong."). Likewise, just as the scrapbooker realized she had no photographs of the Aboriginal Cultural Park and would need to find the brochure to add to her photographs, teacher-researchers may find that they need to collect additional data to inform an emerging pattern. Finally, like the scrapbooker who decided to regroup some pictures into new piles called "Family Stays" and "Assorted Candids," as teacher-researchers' findings emerge, they may regroup, rename, expand, or condense the original ways they grouped their data.

Data Analysis Step Three: Interpretation

Just as the scrapbook teacher invited her student to create her first page by writing a statement that expressed the meaning a group of pictures held for her, in this phase, patterns or themes yield statements about what a teacher-researcher learned and what the learning means. To facilitate this process, you might direct your PLC members to look at the patterns they coded in Step Two, and pose the following questions:

What was your initial wondering and how do these patterns inform it?

What is happening in each pattern and across patterns?

How is what is happening connected to . . .
  a. your teaching?
  b. your students?
  c. the subject matter and your curriculum?
  d. your classroom/school context?

The findings from this step can be illustrated by the teacher-inquirer in a number of ways, including but not limited to themes, patterns, categories, metaphors, simile, claims/assertions, typologies, and vignettes. Figure 5.2 provides a definition of these possible illustrative techniques, as well as examples.

These strategies help illustrate, organize, and communicate inquiry findings to an audience. Once teacher-researchers have outlined their organizing strategy, they will need to identify the data that supports each finding presented in the outline. Excerpts from these data sources will be used as evidence for their claims.

Data Analysis Step Four: Implications

Finally, upon completing each of the three previous steps, teacher-inquirers must draw implications from their learning. To facilitate this process, you might pose the following questions to members of your PLC:

What have you learned about yourself as a teacher?

What have you learned about children?

What have you learned about the larger context of schools and schooling?

What are the implications of what you have learned for your teaching?

What changes might you make to your practice?

What new wonderings do you have?

Figure 5.2 Strategies for Illustrating Your Findings

1. **Themes/Patterns/Categories/Labels/Naming.** A composite of traits or features; a topic for discourse or discussion; a specifically defined division; a descriptive term; set apart from others.
   Example: Collaboration, ownership, care, growth

2. **Metaphors.** A term that is transferred from the object it ordinarily represents to an object it represents only by implicit comparison or analogy.
   Example: the Illustrator, the Translater, the Reporter, the Guide, Casting the Play

3. **Simile.** Two unlike things are compared, often in a phrase introduced by *like* or *as*.
   Example: Music as a motivator, music as a confidence builder, music as a context for making meaningful connections, writing as conversation

4. **Claims/Assertions.** A statement of fact or assertion of truth.
   Example: Inappropriate expectations discouraged many of the learners in my classroom and hindered my effectiveness as a writing teacher.

5. **Typologies.** A systematic classification of types.
   Example: Different uses for puppets: instructional, entertainment, therapeutic

6. **Vignettes.** A brief descriptive literary sketch.
   Example: "The Struggle for Power; Who Is in Control"
   The children were engaged in conversation at the meetings, jobs were continuing to get done, but there was still a struggle centering around who was in control. With the way the class decided to make a list of jobs, break the jobs up into groups, choose the people they wanted to work with, there were breaks in communication. Conflicts were arising with the groups. Everyone was mostly aiming to get "their own" way.

These questions call for teacher-researchers to interpret what they have learned, to take action for change based on their study, and to generate new questions. For, unlike the scrapbooker who can marvel at her completed book, the scrapbook for a teacher-inquirer is never quite finished, even after intensive analysis. Hubbard and Power (1999) note that, "Good research analyses raise more questions than they answer" (p. 117). While teachers may never be able to marvel at a perfected, polished, definitive set of findings based on the data analysis from one particular inquiry, they can marvel at the enormity of what they have learned through engaging in the process, and the power it holds for transforming both their identity as a teacher, as well as their teaching practice. Cochran-Smith and Lytle (2001) propose that:

> a legitimate and essential purpose of professional development is the development of an inquiry stance on teaching that is critical and transformative, a stance linked not only to high standards for the learning of all students but also to social change and social justice and to the individual and collective growth of teachers. (p. 46)

As a result of data analysis, be sure to take the time to allow PLC members to marvel at their growth, and the impact they can have as individual teachers who have joined a PLC, as well as a larger community of teacher-researchers. Through engagement in inquiry as a member of this community, you and the teachers you coach are contributing to the transformation of the teaching profession itself!

COACHING ANALYSIS: THE DATA ANALYSIS MEETING

If members of your PLC have been engaged in one collaborative inquiry during the school year, you have likely already had a number of meetings that occurred after your inquiry brief meeting, during which time you looked at data collected at different points along the way. After a series of these meetings in which you looked closely at individual pieces of data, you will reach a point where all data collection for the entire inquiry has been completed. At this time, it is a good idea to dedicate one entire meeting (often for an extended time) to the data analysis process.

For example, let's return to Kevin, the PLC coach introduced in Chapter 4, and his learning community's inquiry focused on creating more culturally responsive teaching for the students in their school. Early in their inquiry, the group administered a survey to all of the teachers in their building to capture their thoughts about culturally responsive teaching as well as their students' needs. At one of the PLC meetings, Kevin used a protocol called "Chalk Talk" (NSRF, 2007) to facilitate the discussion of the survey data.

The first ten minutes of the meeting was devoted to each PLC member reading through the typed-up responses to the surveys. Next, Kevin briefly explained that they were going to engage in a "chalk talk" to generate ideas about the survey responses. This was a silent activity— no one was to talk and anyone could add to the chalk talk as they pleased by commenting on other people's ideas simply by drawing a connecting line to the comment. In essence, rather than engaging in conversation with spoken words, they were to engage in conversation with words written on paper. Next, Kevin hung up a large roll of chart paper and gave everyone in the group a marker. He wrote the following question in a big circle in the center of the chart paper, "What did you learn from reading the survey responses?" For twenty-five minutes, individuals silently took turns writing on the chart paper about responses that surprised them, responses that confirmed their dissatisfaction with the current state of inclusive practices in their building, and responses that gave direction for their future. When the chalk talk was done, Kevin rolled up that paper and shared that he would save it to revisit later in their inquiry as they approached final data analysis. Over the next few months, Kevin's PLC continued to collect data to inform their wondering according to their plan, discussing this data at PLC meetings in various ways.

As they were approaching the final third of the school year, PLC membership had completed all of the data collection, and it was time to look at the entire data set as a whole. Kevin facilitated this process by dedicating one PLC meeting to this purpose. Two weeks prior to the date set for that meeting, Kevin made enough copies of all of the data collected for each member of the PLC, placing each different copy in its own notebook. Kevin gave one notebook to each PLC member and requested that all members read through the entire notebook once in preparation for their data analysis meeting.

Together, at this extended two-hour data analysis meeting, Kevin walked the group through each step of the data analysis process—description, sense-making, interpretation, and implications. Through the process, the group articulated findings from the data and drew conclusions they planned to present to their principal and the rest of the faculty the next month.

─────── ●●● ───────

When engaging in one collective inquiry as a learning community as in the case of Kevin described above, one single data set is produced. The PLC coach and membership all read this data set and participate in the four-step process of data analysis together. However, if you are coaching a PLC where members are each engaged in their own individual inquiries, each individual inquiry will generate its own unique data set. Time constraints usually do not permit all members of the PLC to read through every individual's entire data set and go through the four-step process together. For this reason, we have found it is helpful to structure the data analysis meeting as a sharing and feedback session, in which each member of the PLC comes to that meeting having already gone through one or more of the steps in the data analysis process on his or her own. During the data analysis meeting, individuals present to the group what they are learning from their data so far. We have developed a protocol (Figure 5.3) to focus each individual and to be sure that everyone in the group gets equal time for sharing and feedback. If your PLC has more than five members, we suggest you break into groups of three or four to engage with this protocol, or hold two separate data analysis feedback meetings with half of your group presenting during the first meeting and the other half presenting at the second. We have found that it is also helpful to have presenting individuals spend about five minutes completing a sentence-completion activity (Figure 5.4) prior to beginning the protocol to help them organize their thoughts.

We end this chapter with a glimpse at the way this protocol might play out in practice through the story of Chris, an eleventh grade English teacher, and his PLC coach, Leanne.

─────── ●●● ───────

Figure 5.3 Data Analysis Protocol

**Data Analysis Protocol:
Helping Your Colleagues Make Sense of What They Learned**

Suggested Group Size: 4
Suggested Time Frame: 25–30 MINUTES PER GROUP MEMBER

Step One: Presenter Shares His or Her Inquiry [four minutes]—Presenter briefly shares with group members the focus or purpose of the inquiry, what his or her wonderings were, how data were collected, and the initial sense that the presenter has made of his or her data. Completing the following sentences prior to discussion may help presenter organize his or her thoughts prior to sharing:

- The issue/dilemma/problem/interest that led me to my inquiry was . . .
- Therefore, the purpose of my inquiry was to . . .
- My wonderings were . . .
- I collected data by . . .
- So far, three discoveries I've made from reading through my data are . . .

Step Two: Group Members Ask Clarifying Questions [three minutes]—Group members ask questions that have factual answers to clarify their understanding of the inquiry, such as, "For how long did you collect data?" "How many students did you work with?"

Step Three: Group Members Ask Probing Questions [seven to ten minutes]—The group then asks probing questions of the presenter. These questions are worded so that they help the presenter clarify and expand his or her thinking about what he or she is learning from the data. During this ten-minute time frame, the presenter may respond to the group's questions, *but there is no discussion by the group of the presenter's responses.* Every member of the group should pose at least one question of the presenter. Some examples of probing questions might include:

a. What are some ways you might organize your data? (See Figure 5.1)
b. What might be some powerful ways to present your data? (See Figure 5.2)
c. Do you have any data that doesn't seem to fit?
d. Based on your data, what are you learning about yourself as a teacher?
e. What is your data telling you about the students you teach?
f. What are the implications of your findings for the content you teach?
g. What have you learned about the larger context of schools and schooling?
h. What are the implications of what you have learned for your teaching?
i. What changes might you make in your own practice?
j. What new wonderings do you have?

Step Four: Group Members Discuss the Data Analysis [six minutes]—The group talks with each other about the data analysis presented, discussing such questions as, "What did we hear?" "What didn't we hear that we think might be relevant?" "What assumptions seem to be operating?" "Does any data not seem to fit with the presenter's analysis?" "What might be some additional ways to look at the presenter's data?" During this discussion, members of the group work to deepen the data analysis. *The presenter doesn't speak during this discussion, but instead listens and takes notes.*

Step Five: Presenter Reflection [three minutes]—The presenter reflects on what he or she heard and what he or she is now thinking, sharing with the group anything that particularly resonated for him or her during any part of the group members' data analysis discussion.

Step Six: Reflection on the Process [two minutes]—Group shares thoughts about how the discussion worked for the group.

SOURCE: Developed by Nancy Fichtman Dana and Diane Yendol-Hoppey.

Figure 5.4 Sentence Completion Activity

The issue/tension/dilemma/problem/interest that led me to my inquiry was

_____

_____

_____

Therefore, the purpose of my inquiry was to _____

_____

_____

My wondering(s) were _____

_____

_____

I collected data by _____

_____

So far, three discoveries I've made from reading through my data are:

(1) _____

_____

_____

(2) _____

_____

_____

(3) _____

_____

_____

Over the past several years, Chris had developed a passion for technology. As an early adopter, he was one of the first to own his own Palm Pilot and the latest smart phone, and to develop his own Web site. As he both enjoyed and benefited from the personal use of technology, through the years, he slowly introduced a number of technological advances into his instruction of American literature for high school juniors. He believed that the meaningful integration of technology into his instruction held promise for adding variety to the traditional literature discussions he held in the classroom, and enriching students' understandings of the great American novels they covered in eleventh grade.

Chris was in his first year as a member of a PLC at his school. Chris became a member of this group at the suggestion of his principal, and found membership in this group to be a painless way to earn the professional development points required by the state to renew his teaching license. Unlike previous professional development sit-and-get workshops, he actually was enjoying the PLC experience and the support he was receiving from other teachers in the completion of a teacher inquiry project focused on his technology passion. For his research this year, Chris was exploring the use of Weblogs with his Honors/AP students to discuss the novel *Moby Dick.*

To gain insights into the ways blogging might enhance in-class discussions, Chris set up a site, reviewed students' posts, and developed a questionnaire students completed focused on their perceptions of the blogging experience. Chris also saved all of his lesson plans and in-class work students completed throughout the *Moby Dick* unit. Chris developed a series of "blog prompts" to initiate the students' participation on the site, and sometimes assigned responding to the prompt as homework.

He had been collecting data for some time, when his PLC coach, Leanne, suggested they devote their next meeting to helping each other begin the process of data analysis. Chris was to read through all of the data he had collected so far, and complete a sheet of open-ended statements (Figure 5.4) to prepare for their next meeting.

Leanne began this meeting by encouraging everyone to take one of her famous brownies she had brought to share. She then handed out the data analysis protocol (Figure 5.3) and reviewed the protocol procedures with the group. She stated, "I know many of you are at a point where you've collected a ton of data, and I think this exercise could really help each of you clarify what your data might be telling you, and where you might go next in your inquiry. Who would like to present first?"

Chris volunteered, "I'll go, although I'm not sure you all can help me too much. You see I feel like I'm not really learning anything from my data—this whole blog experience I set out to do isn't really going as I had hoped."

"Thanks for volunteering, Chris. Let's follow the protocol and see what happens. You'll have four minutes to share with us where you are with your inquiry. You can use the sentence completion sheet you filled out to help you share about your inquiry in a succinct manner. Four minutes goes quickly. I'll keep time. Let's begin."

"Okay, I'm ready," Chris began. "Well, as you already know, I'm extremely intrigued with technology. Most recently I've become fascinated with blogging. Every year, when I teach the novel *Moby Dick*, I'm not entirely happy with the nature of the discussions we have in class. Sometimes I just don't know how to get students to participate more, dig a little deeper, and use higher-level thinking skills as we discuss the novel in class. I thought it might be interesting to see if blogging could make a difference. Therefore, the purpose of my study was to understand how Weblogs might support or hinder my students' discussion during class. My wonderings, which you all so brilliantly helped me craft a few months ago, were: 'What happens when I add a blogging component to my unit on *Moby Dick* with my eleventh grade Honors/AP class?' 'In what ways does blogging contribute to my students' understandings of the novel?' And 'What is the relationship between blogging and the application of higher-order thinking skills to literature discussion?'"

Leanne told Chris, "You have one minute remaining," and Chris continued.

"I collected data by setting up a site, printing out, and reading all of the posts, giving out a questionnaire to my students about blogging, and saving every bit of paper produced by me and my students during my teaching of *Moby Dick*. So far, one thing I'm discovering from my data is that students are posting, but not necessarily responding to each other's posts. It's like they use the blog to dump their thoughts out, but no one responds to each other. Another thing I'm discovering is that there is great variety in the quality of responses by the students. A few responses are really thoughtful as well as thought provoking, but most responses are so general I have to wonder if the student even read the assigned chapter. It's definitely not working like I thought it would."

Leanne interjected, "Okay, Chris, I'm going to have to stop you there. It's been four minutes." Leanne addressed the group, "In the next three minutes, we get to ask Chris clarifying questions. As a reminder, these are questions that have factual answers."

During that three minutes, members of the group posed the following four questions that Chris responded to:

1. Can you tell me more about what the site looks like and how it operates?

2. What instructions did you give to your students about how to use the blog site?

3. Are there instructions for the students on the site itself?

4. Have you ensured that all of your students have access to computers to participate?

After Chris's response to the fourth question, Leanne jumped in, "Although I know we may have a few more clarifying questions we might want Chris to answer, it's time for us to shift gears now and ask probing questions. As a reminder, probing questions are worded to help Chris dig deeper into his thinking and his data analysis. One thing to be careful of is disguising a suggestion as a probing question, or disguising your own thinking or opinion as a probing question by starting out with a phrase such as, 'Did you think of trying . . . ?' or 'Did you ever consider that . . .' At this point, we do not want to offer suggestions to Chris, or impose our own thinking on him. Rather, we want to ask questions to help us delve a little deeper into his inquiry and his data. We'll have the opportunity to make suggestions and share our thinking in the next step of this protocol."

Joan began, "What are you looking for when you review the postings?"

Chris answered, "Well, I'm looking for a couple things. First, I'm looking at the responses, kind of with a Bloom's taxonomy eye. What I mean by that is, are they analyzing, synthesizing, and evaluating in their responses to my blog prompts? I'm also looking not just at how I might categorize their responses using Bloom's taxonomy, but looking at their responses for how they might get scored on Florida Writes, our lovely state test. Of course I want these students to do their very best on this. And as I read their responses, I also can't help but consider how that response might be scored on the AP exam too. I haven't been happy with what I've seen so far."

There was a brief pause and Sherri jumped in, "I remember reading *Moby Dick* in high school and it was very difficult reading. I can't say I have fond memories of it. I'm wondering why you chose *Moby Dick*? Are they required to read that text?"

"Well, no, they're not required to read it. We have a list of books from the state that we can choose from, but you don't have to read every book on the list. I chose it because I consider myself a child of the sea—I grew up myself not far from the ocean. I love fishing and adventure stories, and I like the writing style of the author, so I thought it would be a great novel for the kids. I know it's a challenging read. There's a good deal of internal dialogue the kids have to get through. There's usually a bunch of groans when I first introduce the book. The kids give me a look as if to say, 'Are you kidding me?' But I like the book, and I think it's good for them!"

Sherri responded, "Did you ever think that it might be difficult for the students to relate to this novel and because they can't relate and it provides some difficult content, their blogs aren't up to par?"

Leanne interjected, "Hold on a minute. Let me stop everyone for a second. Sherri, that's one of those disguised questions—you're really giving Chris your own ideas in the way that question is phrased. Hold onto your own thoughts for the next step, and let's keep our questions open. Could anyone reword Sherri's question so it's a probing question and not a suggestion for Chris?"

Mickie said, "I'll give it a try. Chris, what factors might contribute to your students' ability (or inability) to produce quality blog entries?"

Chris responded, "Wow, that's a great question, Mickie. One factor could be the direction for the blog assignment itself. If the directions aren't clear, that could affect the quality. Another thing I suppose is me being explicit about what I'm looking for in their entries. Since I'm new to using blogging, I think I had in my head what I wanted to see, but I'm not sure I communicated it well to the students. I guess I also might see more quality blog activity if the content wasn't so difficult, but that's a catch-22 situation. I thought the blog activity would be good just for that reason—it would give the students yet another venue to deconstruct a difficult text. I'll have to think about that some more."

Leanne took a turn probing, "Chris, you said that one of the things you are looking for in their prompts is higher-order thinking skills. What have you done with your students to help them understand higher-order thinking?"

"Well, I've done some instruction with topic sentences, and various activities to help them build on those sentences." Chris stopped and thought for a minute. "I don't think I'm answering your question. In reality, Leanne, I don't think I've done much to scaffold their learning and application of higher-order thinking from other class activities to the blog activity."

Joan was next, "What implications does what you are learning from your data have for your teaching?"

Chris responded, "I am definitely seeing adaptations I could make to the ways I designed the site so it is more effective. I also just assumed that because these kids were eleventh grade Honors/AP students they would really take off with the blogging, you know, like a duck takes to water. Being bright students, I also assumed that their blogs would be so thought provoking that they would automatically be compelled to respond to each other. Those were naive assumptions on my part. You would think that after so many years teaching I would have known better. I can't just teach the content *Moby Dick,* I have to teach the technology too. I need to teach them what constitutes a quality blog entry, and perhaps not only what constitutes a quality blog entry, but a quality response to a peer's blog."

Leanne finished up with the final question, "Chris, we have time for only one more question, and I think a good one to finish up might be, 'What new wonderings do you have?'"

"There's a lot of things swirling around in my head right now, but one thing that's coming to mind is the development of a rubric for blog responses. If I developed a rubric, I'd want to know the relationship between the rubric and the students' ability to produce blog responses that are indicative of higher-order thinking."

"Okay, thanks Chris. At this point, we're going to move on to the next step in the protocol. Chris, we are now going to discuss your inquiry with each other, as if you weren't in the room. You are to remain silent. You might want to take notes as we talk. You also might want to scoot your chair back a little from our circle and turn away from us just a tad to help you resist the urge to contribute to the discussion."

Chris scooted his chair back from the group as Leanne suggested, and took out his notepad, ready to write. Leanne continued by addressing the group, "We are going to talk about Chris' data for six minutes. We should discuss questions such as: 'What did we hear?' 'What didn't we hear that we think might be relevant?' 'What assumptions seem to be operating?' 'Does any data not seem to fit with the presenter's analysis?' And, 'What might be some additional ways to look at the presenter's data?' What we're trying to do is deepen Chris' analysis. And Sherri, here's the time you could make suggestions."

Joan began, "I hear Chris say that when analyzing his students' blog entries, he was looking for the higher levels of Bloom's taxonomy in their responses, and most of the responses were not at those higher-order thinking levels. I wonder if Chris made this statement based on his impressions over time, or if he actually sorted his data by Bloom taxonomy level. He might want to actually sort the blog entries into the categories of knowledge, comprehension, application, analysis, synthesis, and evaluation. He also might want to sort his blog prompts into these categories as well. He might discover some interesting things by sorting his data this way. Maybe it's not as bad as he thinks. Maybe the prompts themselves aren't all higher-level questions. Are knowledge, comprehension, and application questions inherently bad? Especially for a difficult novel like *Moby Dick*, I would imagine the students would need to spend some time in the knowledge, comprehension, and application domains before they can discuss the text at a higher level."

Mickie continued, "I also hear Chris say that he was looking at the responses for how they might get scored on the Florida Writes and the AP exam. That was puzzling to me, because I heard nothing in Chris' wondering statements that had to do with student writing. In all the discussions we had about his inquiry at previous meetings, I never remember hearing anything about Florida Writes or the AP exam. Did you?"

Members of the PLC shook their heads.

"This writing thing is totally new. He needs to return to his wonderings to remind himself of what he set out to look for in the first place. He didn't ask, 'How does blogging help students prepare for Florida Writes and the AP test?'"

Joan spoke, "Along with that, I was thinking that his students were perceiving the blog site like they might perceive MySpace, or Facebook, or Instant Messenger. They write in a much more informal way in these venues. Why would you expect they'd write like they would for an exam on a blog site?"

Members of the PLC nodded in agreement. Leanne shared, "I think an important part of his data analysis is going to be looking very closely at all of his lesson plans and everything that went into designing the blog site itself. He might want to turn his gaze to focus on the set up—What did I learn from the way I set it all up? What worked? What didn't?"

Mickie said, "I didn't hear him talk at all about the questionnaires. Did he look at them yet or did he only look at the blog entries themselves?"

Sherri continued, "Alright, I've been quiet long enough. I have to come back to his choice of *Moby Dick*. I can't imagine that's an easy book for the kids to relate to, and that certainly could inhibit their responses. Maybe Chris should try a more accessible novel for eleventh graders in the future. I know they're Honors/AP students, but *Moby Dick?* There may be better choices on that list from the state."

"Does Chris have to be the one to pick from that list? What would happen if he did a little two-minute commercial on each book on the list, and then his students could vote on the one they want to read," suggested Mickie.

Joan chimed in, "Or, each individual student could pick the book he or she wanted and Chris could make book blog groups. Does everyone in the class have to be reading the same book at the same time?"

There was a pause while everyone thought. Leanne took this opportunity to look down at her watch and broke the silence with, "We have two minutes left."

Joan continued, "I think Chris uncovered some of his own assumptions when he was speaking. For instance, Chris noted that just because they were bright kids, he thought they'd take to blogging like ducks take to water."

Leanne elaborated, "He also thought they'd respond to each other naturally."

"I think this is one thing he might take into consideration in the design of the blog and his directions for its use," Sherri recommended. "Maybe the kids need to be required not just to post, but to respond to at least three classmate's blog posts by a certain date . . . or something like that."

Joan expressed concern, "I worry that Chris is beating up on himself too hard for making some assumptions about advanced learners. He even started out by saying that he didn't think he was learning much from his inquiry since the blogging was not going as he had planned. Well gosh, I think he's learning an incredible amount. One thing he is learning is that we all make assumptions based on ability when we plan our lessons. Sometimes the assumptions we make limit our planning. This could even be one of the claims he makes in his findings . . . something like, 'It is important for teachers to uncover hidden assumptions they hold about their learners that may interfere with the teacher's ability to introduce something new to the class.' I know I was thinking about that as he was talking. His inquiry helped me look at myself and the assumptions I make as well. The practice of uncovering our assumptions is a good reminder for us all!"

Leanne agreed, "I think that's really powerful. It's important to remember that engaging in teacher research isn't about finding a new strategy and reporting on the miraculous difference it made to teaching. Although that does happen occasionally, more often that not, teaching is just too complex to have any one new thing a teacher might try in the classroom lead to dramatic improvement for every learner in a short period of time. But, that doesn't mean that there isn't tons of learning that happens through each inquiry cycle. It seems like Chris has a lot of rich learning to report on! And with that comment, I'm going to have to call time and ask Chris to come back and join us in the circle. Chris, you now have three minutes to reflect on what you heard us say."

"Wow, this was incredible. I have three full pages of notes. Let me just share a few things. First, I really like the idea of sorting the blog entries and prompts by taxonomy level. I haven't done that yet. I do think that would be an interesting exercise. I was thinking it's all about higher-level thinking and that's the only valuable blog response to have. Once I sort, I think I might find some value in using the blog for knowledge, comprehension, and application as well as analysis, synthesis and evaluation. I'm going to go through my data again and look closely at what exactly is happening at each of those levels, as well as how the lower level responses might be building blocks for the higher-level responses.

"I also want to say that you're right on about the Florida Writes and the AP test. That did just seem to creep into my inquiry. I think that probably happen because we're getting close to the end of the year, and of course, just like everyone, those tests and my students' performance on them is ever present on my mind. This wasn't the focus of my study, though, so I need to let that one go. There's no need to sort my data by the score a response like that would receive on the exams.

"I do think there's something to the students' application of MySpace, Facebook, and instant messaging behaviors to the blog space. I think I even might want to do a few interviews with certain students to see if they perceive my blog site in the same ways they perceive all those social networking sites—wow, that could have some powerful implications for how I adapt my blog site in the future, as well as the instructions I give about participation on the site.

"And I have administered and collected the questionnaires, but I just glanced at them. So far, I've really focused my analysis on just the blog entries themselves. I have to go back to my data and look at the questionnaires more closely.

"I have a lot more to say, but Leanne is giving me the time signal, so I just want to thank everyone. I have to admit, I was really skeptical about this whole protocol thing and data analysis at first, but this session has been incredibly helpful. I have so much to consider! Thanks."

Leanne responded with a smile, "Thank you, Chris. You were brave to present first. We will now take just two minutes to reflect on the process."

Mickie said, "For lack of a better word, this was really cool. The protocol worked well. It kept us focused and on topic, and the time moved quickly."

Sherri added, "I think it's hard to distinguish between suggestions and probing questions. I know I had a hard time with that, but when Mickie rephrased my question, I did see that difference, and why it is important to make sure a question is a true probing question and not a suggestion disguised as a probing question."

Leanne responded, "It's not easy to develop good probing questions, but it's a skill we'll all get better at with time."

Joan said, "It felt a little weird talking about Chris as if he wasn't in the room when he was sitting right next to me." Everyone chuckled.

Chris shared, "You think it felt weird to you—I'm glad I took Leanne's suggestion and pulled away from the circle a bit. There were so many times I wanted to say something when you were discussing me. I'm glad the protocol wouldn't let me though. I learned so much by just listening!"

Leanne finished up, "That's time! Let's take a quick five minute break and then Joan, why don't you present next?"

The members of the learning community relaxed. Chris helped himself to a second brownie, Sherri went to the restroom, Mickie purchased a soda, and Joan engaged in some quiet conversation with Leanne as they waited for the others to return. While they momentarily went their separate ways, each member of the learning community had experienced the power of protocols that afternoon, as well as the power teacher inquiry and the data analysis process holds for teacher learning. They eagerly awaited the next round.

6

Helping
PLC Members
Share Their
Work With Others

A young man took his thirteen-year-old son to the lake. He was look-ing forward to spending the beautiful spring day making fond mem-ories with his son, who was growing much too quickly for his father's comfort. The weather was perfect—the sun was warm, and the air was fresh with just a little nip of cold remaining from the long winter months. Because it was early spring, they had the entire park to themselves, not another family was in sight.

The day was going just as the young father had planned. After the perfect morning canoe trip, they headed to the shore and ate their picnic lunch. After lunch, the man gazed out and admired the peace-ful, calm lake before him. His thoughts drifted to replaying the won-derful morning he and his son had shared together, and he was feeling quite proud of the all-day excursion he had planned for his son during these delicate teenage years—it couldn't have been going any better. Just then, his thoughts were abruptly interrupted by his child's voice: "Dad, I'm bored."

The man was taken aback—stunned that his son could feel boredom in the face of the beautiful glassy-still lake before them. "How could you be bored, son?" his father queried. "The lake is so beautiful—peaceful and still."

"That's just it, Dad," his son replied. "You might see beauty, but I see stagnation." His son's comment provided a stark reality check for the man—they had sat for too long, and he needed to think quickly to save the perfect day he had planned with his son from spoiling.

"Son," his father said, "I think it's time to put an end to the stagnation. You see all of these rocks along the shore? Have I ever told you I was my town's rock-skipping champion when I was a kid? I can give you a few pointers, and teach you how to skip rocks like nobody's business!"

The teenaged boy looked skeptical. "Aw Dad, I'm too old for that stuff."

"You're never too old to have fun and to learn something new. Now watch me."

The man searched for the perfect rock on the lake shore, and tossed it into the water. It skipped three times before it finally fell to the bottom. Its hops across the water's surface created an interesting pattern of ripples.

While the boy didn't want to admit it, he was impressed. He watched his father throw five more rocks in quick succession—one even skipped four times! He decided since no one was in sight to see him, it would be okay to participate with his father.

They threw for an hour, his father teaching him technique and form to get as many skips as possible out of each rock. As they tossed stone after stone, the clear, stagnant lake came alive with small swells, ridges, and swirls. Some of the ripples even reached the shore of the lake! The man was once again proud of his quick thinking—the stone throwing game had saved the day.

Like the stones laying on the lake shore that have no chance of impacting the still water unless tossed in by the man and his teenaged son, an unshared inquiry has little chance of changing practice unless that inquiry is tossed into the professional conversation and dialogue that contributes to the knowledge base for teaching. Once tossed in, it disturbs the status quo of educational practices, creating a ripple effect, beginning with the teacher himself or herself, the immediate vicinity (the students and classroom) and emanating out to a school, a district, a state—eventually reaching and contributing to the transformation of the perimeter of all practice—the profession of teaching itself. Hence, one critical component of coaching inquiry within your PLC is helping the teachers you work with "jump into the lake" by sharing their work with others. The purpose of this chapter is to explore several venues for sharing inquiry and to help coaches create spaces for that sharing to occur.

It is important to note that a precursor to teacher sharing often involves alleviating any concerns or trepidation created by the prospect of sharing work with others, many of which are discussed in Chapter 2. Unfortunately, for many years, norms of teacher isolation existed in schools, and part of your work as a coach will be to collaborate with school leaders and teachers to break this mold of isolation. Peter W. Dillon (2007), a MetLife Fellow who writes for the Teacher's Network, notes:

> Traditionally, schools have been isolating places for teachers to work in. Teachers often feel separated from each other. The press of busy schedules, course loads, and additional duties makes it difficult for teachers to make the time to talk never mind work together. Teachers need opportunities to talk and collaborate with each other to best serve their students, to make their work more meaningful, and to transform schooling in a way that keeps it vibrant and relevant.

Because these norms have been so pervasive, it is not uncommon for teachers to feel anxiety about the prospect of sharing their practice with others outside the comfort of the PLC. Like the man encouraging his son, "You're never too old to have fun and learn something new," an inquiry coach must gently encourage and sometimes create the spaces for sharing to occur in a nonthreatening, comfortable, but meaningful way. Encouragement begins by reviewing *why* it's critical to share inquiry work with others.

THE IMPORTANCE OF SHARING: A REVIEW

There are four important benefactors when the teachers in your PLC "jump into the lake" and share their work—the teachers themselves, their students, other teachers, and the profession at large.

For teachers, the process of preparing their findings to share with others helps them to clarify their own thinking about their work. In addition to clarifying their own thinking, in the actual sharing of their work, they give other professionals access to their thinking so that they can question, discuss, debate, and relate. This process helps inquirers and their colleagues push and extend their thinking about practice as well.

Clarifying, pushing, and extending thinking are not the only benefits of sharing. Fellow professionals also benefit from the knowledge a teacher or group of teachers created through engagement in action research. For example, veteran teacher-researcher George Dempsie's passion for using puppets as a form of pedagogy with young children led him to study and publish the results of this practice (Dempsie, 1997, 2000). In his own district, he has inspired puppetry as pedagogy in dozens of teachers, across eleven different elementary buildings. His presentations at conferences and publications allow his work to spread outside his immediate vicinity (classroom, school, district) as well.

Sharing inquiry with other professionals can also change the very ways children experience schooling. For example, we know one teacher who completed an inquiry on an individual second grade child who was having great difficulty fitting into the structure of schooling as it existed socially, but was not receiving any services because she did not qualify in any traditional ways. Her inquiry illuminated many critical insights into the child that traditional forms of assessment would not have generated. Becoming an advocate for this child, the teacher shared the results of her inquiry with other specialists and the principal. Eventually, a full-time paraprofessional was hired to work individually with this child within the regular classroom each school day. In a year's time, the child made great strides forward in her academic and social development.

We have provided just two specific examples here to illustrate the power, and therefore, necessity of sharing inquiry. Some inquiries inspire small, local change. Some inspire large, sweeping change. All change, large or small, is significant in that the changes that are occurring are emanating from those best positioned to make a difference in education, and those that for years have been kept from making that difference—teachers themselves!

Kincheloe (1991) writes about the ways teachers have been kept from making that difference using a comparison between teachers and peasants within a third-world culture with hierarchical power structures, scarce resources, and traditional values:

> Like their third-world counterparts, teachers are preoccupied with daily survival—time for reflection and analysis seems remote and even quite fatuous given the crisis management atmosphere and the immediate attention survival necessitates. In such a climate those who would suggest that more time and resources be delegated to reflective and growth-inducing pursuits are viewed as impractical visionaries devoid of common sense. Thus, the status quo is perpetuated, the endless cycle of underdevelopment rolls on with its peasant culture of low morale and teachers as "reactors" to daily emergencies. (p. 12)

When teachers in your PLC get into the lake and share their inquiries, you and the teachers you coach contribute to breaking the cycle described above. You, and the teachers you coach, contribute to educational reform:

The plethora of small changes made by critical teacher researchers around the world in individual classrooms may bring about far more authentic educational reform than the grandiose policies formulated in state or national capitals. (Kincheloe, 1991, p. 14)

By getting into the lake and sharing your inquiries, you and the teachers you coach contribute to changing the ways some people outside of teaching view teachers and their practice and try to change education from the outside in. In the sharing of your inquiry, you contribute to reforming the profession of teaching—from the inside out!

CREATING A SPACE AND TIME FOR SHARING

In our work, we have witnessed numerous venues that have been constructed for teacher research sharing. In this section, we name the five most common examples we have witnessed—executive summary write-ups, district alternative evaluation plans or professional development plans, PowerPoint presentations, posters, and Weblogs. By naming and describing these venues, we hope to spark your best creative thinking as you ponder ways to provide meaningful contexts for the wonderful work that has occurred within your inquiry-oriented PLC to be packaged and spread, just like the ripples in the lake created by the stones in the story that opened this chapter.

Executive Summary Write-Ups

Some teachers enjoy packaging their research experience and learning in prose describing every detail of their inquiry and the subsequent learning that occurred as a result of engaging in the process. In many cases, these lengthy action research stories become a part of a larger collection of teacher research that is published for others outside of the immediate vicinity of the work to benefit from (see, e.g., Caro-Bruce, Flessner, Klehr, & Zeichner, 2007; Masingila, 2006; Meyers & Rust, 2003).

In many more cases, however, writing is seen as a chore and many teachers experience stress when confronted with the prospect of writing up their work. To alleviate this stress, we have introduced the concept of an *executive summary write-up* into our work at the Center for School Improvement (http://www.coe.ufl.edu/csi) at the University of Florida (Dana & Baker, 2006; Dana & Delane, 2007). Executive summaries provide brief overviews of a teacher's inquiry, as well as contact information for the teacher so more detail about a teacher's work can be shared through personal contact with the author. Executive summaries are generally three to five pages in length and contain the following six components:

- Name of the teacher, title, school, and e-mail address
- Background information (three to five paragraphs that discuss what led the teacher to this inquiry, ending with a statement of the wondering)

- Inquiry design (three to five paragraphs that describe what the teacher did, including data collection and analysis)
- Stating what was learned and resulting changes in practice (five to ten paragraphs that describe what the teacher learned and how his or her practice has changed based on what was learned)
- Providing concluding thoughts (three to five paragraphs stating the implications this research had for the teacher's future practice and stating new wonderings that emerged as a result of engaging in this inquiry)
- References

One example of an executive summary appears at the end of this chapter (Burgin, 2007). Teachers who have written an inquiry brief as described in Chapter 4 have already completed the first two bullets above. Therefore, the first two sections of the inquiry write-up can often be lifted directly from the brief, or modified from the brief if the inquiry has changed over time. When teachers realize that half of their executive summary is already drafted and can be lifted from their inquiry brief, the prospect of sharing their work in writing becomes an even less daunting task.

Working in partnership with the University of Florida (UF) and personnel in the Lastinger Center for Learning, whose mission is to promote sustained, measurable improvement in the academic achievement of Florida's elementary school children in high-poverty schools, Collier County Public Schools introduced the notions of PLCs and teacher inquiry into the work of teachers in Immokalee, an isolated, high-poverty rural community located on the northern edge of the Everglades. Five elementary, one middle, and one high school provide the education for a large population of migrant families in this community. UF faculty members Sylvia Boyton and Alyson Adams worked with Collier County Public Schools staff developer Cathy Gould to organize more than fifty Immokalee teachers into smaller inquiry-oriented PLCs and engage in action research.

Each teacher or team of teachers who engaged in research produced an executive summary of their work, following the model described above. These executive summarizes were organized by topic and compiled into a monograph (Adams, Boynton, Church, & Gould, 2007). Subsequently, the monograph was shared with other teachers in the Collier County School District, outside the community of Immokalee. The monograph not only helped other teachers across the district think about their own practice in relationship to the topics of the inquiries printed in the monograph, but helped to educate these teachers about the process of teacher research as well.

Cathy Gould led her district in capturing the enthusiasm for the inquiry process on DVD, and is using this district-produced DVD along with the monograph to spread the PLC and teacher research work across the entire district.

District Professional Development Plans

Some PLCs have integrated their work into the fabric of the school and school system so that the teachers are provided the opportunity to connect their inquiry work to their professional development plan. A professional development plan is often an alternative evaluation approach that a district uses to document teacher competence and in many cases is more of an effort in compliance rather than a true mechanism that promotes teacher learning. In districts such as Alachua County, Florida, school principals have found ways to integrate the professional development plan into the teacher evaluation system. For example, Jim Brandenburg, the principal at Alachua Elementary School, has worked with the teacher's union and district officials to develop the professional development plan form to accommodate the work of teacher inquiry, making teacher inquiry a part of rather than apart from the work teachers are doing in his school (Brandenburg & Yendol-Hoppey, 2007).

In this case, the teachers' inquiry work is not compiled into one collection within a monograph but rather is summarized using the professional development plan form found at the end of this chapter. Teachers at Alachua Elementary School use this form to share their individual inquiry work with their principal throughout the school year as well as with the members of their PLC.

During the final PLC meeting for the academic year, typically held in late April, the group convenes to review the inquiry findings using the NSRF "A Change in Practice" protocol. Similar to the inquiry brief packaging and sharing, a PLC member makes enough copies of his or her professional development plan for all members of the PLC. Using the protocol to help PLC members deconstruct the inquiry, the PLC divides into triads and spends approximately seventy-five minutes reviewing each other's inquiry. The protocol begins with the presenter distributing a professional development plan and presenting a five to seven minute overview of his or her inquiry. Next, the group members spend about five minutes asking the presenter clarifying questions about the inquiry. After the group finishes clarifying the inquiry work, the group moves to discussing the inquiry. In many cases, the group looks at each step of the inquiry process from creating a wondering, to collecting data, to generating findings in an effort to both share and raise questions about the important work that was completed, to teacher and student learning. The group ends by summarizing "What new insights occurred for all of us as a result of hearing about this particular work?" This small group sharing provides the presenter a space for deeper reflection on the sum of his or her work, as well as moves the work out to a broader audience.

PowerPoint Presentations

Some teachers enjoy packaging their research experience and learning by giving an oral talk. To create a visual component to accompany the oral story of teacher research, many teachers create a series of PowerPoint slides. When a handout of these slides accompany an oral talk about the research, the slides serve to capture the oral story in a way that it can be told and retold many times as teachers refer back to the slides when they consider their own practice in relationship to the presenter. Presentations can be small (a ten-minute talk for the members of the PLC or the building administrative team), medium-sized (a ten-minute talk at a division meeting), or large (a ten- to twenty-minute talk at a faculty meeting).

Mark Bracewell and Rhonda Clyatt, principal and reading coach at Lake Butler Middle School located in Union County, Florida, planned a special extended faculty meeting for their entire school as they neared the end of the year. The purpose of this special faculty meeting was for teachers to share both best practices and action research conducted at Lake Butler that school year.

As reading coach, Rhonda had incorporated the facilitation of action research into her duties as reading coach at the school. She formulated a team of four interested teachers, and they had met monthly over the school year as a learning community to support each other throughout each step in the inquiry process. They were scheduled to present their work to other teachers in North Central Florida at a teacher research conference run by the Center for School Improvement at the University of Florida the last week of April each year. Rhonda lamented that while her PLC members were to share their work with other teachers across the northern part of the state, they had no opportunity to share their work with teachers right in their own building.

As principal, Mark had conducted numerous classroom walk-throughs and was proud of the wonderful practice he had observed during many of these walk-throughs. As he reflected on these walk-throughs, he realized that in his role as principal, he was the only one who got to see some of these outstanding practices at his school enacted, and longed for other teachers in his building to experience his pride in seeing the good work of their teaching colleagues.

Together, Rhonda and Mark planned the Lake Butler Best Practices Showcase for an early-release staff development day in early April. The teachers Rhonda had worked with created PowerPoint presentations of their action research, and Mark sent e-mails to a number of teachers he had been impressed with and asked them to share the particular strategies he had witnessed in their classrooms. After fourteen teachers agreed to participate as presenters, Rhonda obtained a title and a few sentences from each teacher describing what he or she would share, and created a program that was handed out to the entire faculty at the start of their early release day showcase. This program appears at the end of this chapter.

Each presenter took turns sharing his or her work with the entire faculty in seven to ten minute increments. After half of the presenters had shared, the faculty enjoyed a meal together, provided by one of the grade-level teams as is practice during each early-release staff development day at Lake Butler. After their meal, the remaining presenters shared their work.

Rhonda and Mark received very positive feedback from the faculty. In fact, one faculty member shared that this was their best staff development early release day to date! As a result of this afternoon, many teachers expressed a desire to visit the classrooms of their colleagues. Mark set a goal for himself to get teachers into each other's classrooms the following school year.

Posters

Some teachers enjoy packaging their research experience and learning using a poster that can be presented to the PLC members, to the school faculty, or in some other district forum. For example, teachers and prospective teachers at Alachua Elementary School have created a space that looks much like a science fair where inquiry posters are set up around the media center during an early-release day at the end of the school year. Figure 6.1 shows one example of a poster completed by an Alachua Elementary teacher.

The faculty, comprised of thirty-six teacher-inquirers, are divided into four groups of nine presenters and each group is given a thirty-minute time slot for presenting their posters to the rest of the faculty. The audience move from poster to poster asking the poster presenters questions about the inquiry work. The inquiry poster fair typically consists of two rounds of sharing and then a break for refreshments. The refreshment break is followed by two more rounds of sharing and then the teachers are asked to submit a reflection sheet that they had been making notations on throughout the afternoon. The reflection sheet summarizes their learning as a result of both their own presentation as well as their review of others' presentations.

One way that the Alachua teachers recognize the value of the inquiry fair is that most teachers don't run out of the media center as soon as the sessions conclude but rather many stay and discuss interesting ideas they were contemplating as a result of their participation. These opportunities to hear about each other's work during the poster sessions generate conversation beyond the inquiry fair as teachers become more familiar with each other's interests and work.

Weblogs

Some teachers enjoy packaging their research experience and learning using technology. For example, some teacher-researchers are using blogs, typically written and displayed in chronological order, to share their inquiry work with other educators. One teacher, Barbara, used a blog to document and share her reflections as she explored the following question: "How does technology actually change the way students think?"

Barbara posted her progress during each stage of her inquiry, and the members of her inquiry network would provide feedback and questioning that helped her deepen her inquiry work. By the end of the year, Barbara could not only provide documentation that illustrated each step of her inquiry work and her reflections on each stage, but she could also identify

Figure 6.1 Sample Poster

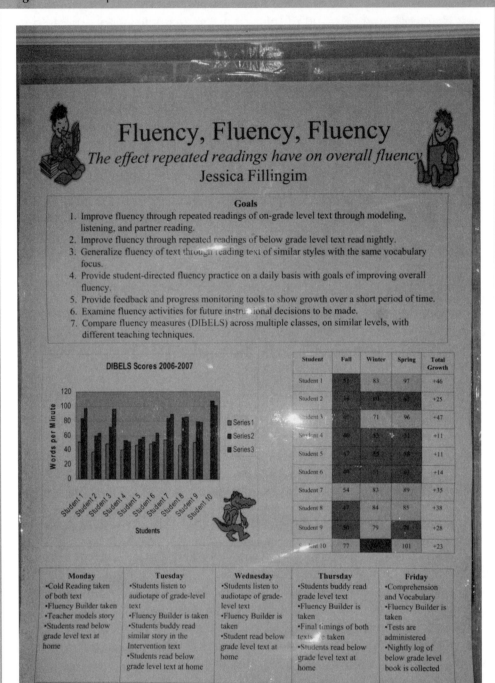

the types of feedback she received from other group members that prompted deeper thinking and changes in her teaching. In addition to providing Barbara with a vehicle to document her inquiry process, the blog also allowed her to share the key findings from her inquiry related to technology with an audience that extended far beyond the school community as she networked with other educators from around the world.

SHARING PLC INQUIRY WORK WITH A LARGER AUDIENCE

In addition to using the five venues named above to create in-school and in-district sharing opportunities for the teachers you work with, in your role as inquiry-oriented PLC coach, you might also suggest that the teachers you have worked with share their work with larger audiences by submitting work to journals and/or state and national conferences. There are many structures in place that coaches can help make teachers aware of as vehicles for sharing teacher inquiry work with an audience outside of their school.

Today, an increasing number of journals and conference forums are designed with a teacher-researcher audience in mind. These include *Teacher Research: The Journal of Classroom Inquiry*, and *Teaching and Learning: The Journal of Naturalistic Inquiry*. Additionally, you can share your written work online by exploring one of the many actions research Web sites, listservs, and online journals. Mills (2003) identifies the following Web sites as useful to those interested in sharing their teacher research: *Educational Action Research* at http://www.tandf.co.uk/journals/titles/09650792.asp, *Networks* at http://journals.library.wisc.edu/index.php/networks, *Action Research International* at http://www.scu.edu.au/schools/gcm/ar/ari/arihome .html, *Action Research Electronic Reader* at http://www.scu.edu.au/ schools/gcm/ar/arr/arow/default.html, and *Centre for Action Research in Professional Practice* at http://www.bath.ac.uk/carpp.

In addition to these forums, teacher-researchers can become involved in special interest groups (SIGs) that are a part of the American Educational Research Association (AERA), perhaps the largest and most well-known education organization. AERA offers membership in a Teacher as Researcher special interest group, as well as a special interest group focused on Professional Development Schools, where a good amount of action research is completed each year. More information about these groups can be found at http://www.aera.net/. In addition to the Professional Development School SIG, given that substantial attention is given to teacher inquiry by professional development schools, teachers who engage in inquiry as a part of their work in professional development schools might benefit from presenting their work at the National Association of Professional Development School (NAPDS) Conference or preparing a manuscript for the NAPDS journal. More information about NAPDS can be found at http://napds.org/.

Figure 6.2 Four Cs of Sharing

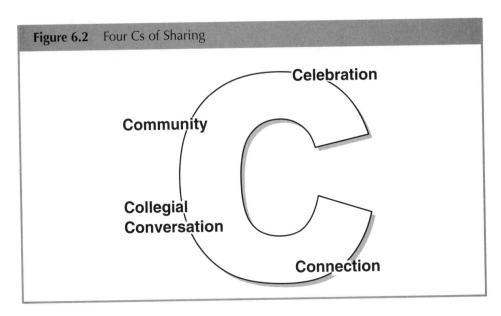

Finally, the International Conference for Teacher Research (ICTR), a small conference that occurs each April right after the annual meeting of AERA, seeks to promote practitioner research among educators, and to foster conversations among academics and classroom teachers. More information about ICTR can be found at http://www.nl.edu/academics/nce/ictr.cfm.

FOUR CORE COMPONENTS OF SHARING

Whatever venues you and the teachers you work with use for the sharing work, coaches need to pay attention to four critical components as they determine the best process for sharing the inquiry work within their context. The four components, summarized in Figure 6.2, titled "Four Cs of Sharing," include *Celebration, Community, Collegial Conversation,* and *Connections.*

Celebration

First and foremost, all sharing should be completed in the spirit of celebration. Communities develop celebrations as rituals for highlighting the success of their individual and collective work. Celebrations provide the opportunity for educators to gather together to mark an accomplishment, as well as make that accomplishment widely known to others. By organizing a celebration for the inquiry work, you will help create roles, rituals, and symbols that call attention to the importance of teacher learning within your community. The celebration helps to communicate a vision for teacher learning. Many PLCs enhance these celebrations by having beverages and food, providing a token of accomplishment in the form of a pin or certificate, and/or having inspirational speakers. You should be thinking about these extra touches as you plan these settings for sharing!

Community

It is important to remember that one of the three words the acronym PLC stands for is community! The word *community* can be defined as a group of people with a common background who possess a shared, common interest. In the case of your PLC, you are working with participants who share the common background of devoting their lives to education and they share the common interest to improve schools and continually learn more about the teaching and learning process. In relationship to sharing, however, community also means developing a sense of trust and connection to others within the group, and creating a space that enables group members to feel good about the work they have accomplished over the course of the year—wrestling with identifying a common intent, shared beliefs, and useful resources, as well as identifying individual and collective preferences and needs for PLC work.

Sharing sessions that review these activities help the definition of *community* in PLC represent not just a group of people who gather together with common background and interest, but represent that your PLC has developed a *sense of community*. A sense of community is characterized by the individuals within your PLC exhibiting care and concern for one another as they share their work and/or become an audience for PLC members who are sharing. A sense of community is also characterized by individuals expressing a feeling of belonging to the group and the PLC work. For this reason, sharing sessions ought to promote a reminder of the critical importance of PLC work and teachers' engagement in inquiry, and promote a feeling that PLC members are proud to be a part of the work that the group completed. When attention is given to developing a sense of community during sharing, PLC participants begin to develop an identity as a teacher-inquirer and see that their work as an educator is far-reaching. In a profession that is fraught with daily struggles and challenges, reminders of what the teaching profession and PLC work is all about help teachers feel good about themselves and become inspired to continue the work of inquiry-oriented PLCs.

Collegial Conversations

Although the first two Cs of sharing (celebration and community) work together during sharing sessions to help teachers feel good about their learning, collegial conversations are critical to making a PLC's sharing sessions a successful learning experience for all. Recall in Chapter 2 our discussion about the difference between congeniality and collegiality. Congenial conversation is the type of conversation that occurs when people enjoy each other's company—talking about family, television, upcoming social events. In contrast, collegial conversations are the types of conversation that occur when teachers focus on their practice, and participants in the dialogue feel compelled to ask each other probing questions, look at their practices from multiple perspectives, and collaboratively shape new meanings together. While creating a spirit of celebration and community are extremely important, the danger of focusing on celebration and community is that sharing, in whatever form it takes, becomes congenial rather than collegial. A sharing session ought to promote collegial questioning and conversation, not just congenial commentary such as "Wow, great work!" Celebrations that embrace collegiality will make your PLC thrive, becoming a synergistic space for all participants to learn.

Connections

In addition to creating a celebratory feel, developing a sense of community, and encouraging collegial conversations during sharing, sharing should be organized so that teachers can network and connect with others who are interested in the same ideas. By connecting their work to others, the participants can generate localized and shared knowledge rather than creating an unsystematic piling up of teacher research. A part of your coaching work needs to focus on establishing ways to enhance teacher networks both internally and externally to your school context.

Each of the four Cs described in this section are critical components of an inquiry culture, the kind of culture that you will want to foster as you coach your PLC. Within an inquiry culture, each inquiry builds on another, leading to deep changes in teacher and student learning. Linda, a teacher collaboration specialist, described the importance of creating a culture of inquiry on the Teacher Leaders Network (2007):

> Ideally, part of the transition process and reform of the schools is the idea of collaborative inquiry—learning together about issues, about the work that teachers identify that they feel passionate about pursuing. This way, everyone takes a learning stance. Norms are key, so that we learn to treat each other as partners, with everyone having skills, knowledge, and pieces of the whole to offer. As we work together over time, trust will be built through learning together on behalf of our students and our profession.

Linda's reflection highlights how a culture of collaborative inquiry can fuel the work of teacher inquirers. Coaching the sharing of inquiry helps create this culture!

SAMPLE ACTION RESEARCH WRITE-UP

A Demo-a-Day in High School Chemistry
Stephen Burgin, Chemistry Teacher
P.K. Yonge Developmental Research School
sburgin@pky.ufl.edu

Background

As a high school chemistry teacher, I have been constantly distressed by the apparent fright that accompanies the typical high school student's enrollment in my introductory chemistry course. What is it about chemistry that makes it so seemingly "impossible" for so many students? Sometimes it feels as if a student's belief that he or she will fail at chemistry becomes a self-fulfilling prophecy. My personal study of chemistry came with no such fears. What was it about my experiences that got me excited and even passionate about this subject? Thinking back to my high school and college chemistry courses, the use of demonstrations was the one thing that most enthralled me. I can still remember most of the demonstrations that I saw as a high school student. These "magic tricks" were one of the reasons I decided to major in chemistry in college. The anticipation of being able to perform them one day in a classroom of my own was a key motivating factor for me in becoming a high school chemistry teacher.

Looking into the research on lecture demonstrations yielded some very interesting discoveries. I found that many educators are apprehensive about performing demonstrations for a number of reasons. Some believe that demonstrations are too costly for their science department. Others feel that demonstrations are too exhausting to execute or too time-consuming to prepare. The most surprising find was that research on the connections between lecture demonstrations and student achievement is so limited that educators don't feel like an extensive use of such demonstrations is warranted (Meyer, Schmidt, Nozawa, Panee, & Kisler, 2003). However, the pedagogical reasons for performing demonstrations given by Meyer, et al., (2003) are much more numerous. Demonstrations provide students with learning opportunities that would be otherwise impossible. Doing demonstrations allows students to visualize experiences that would not be feasible in a laboratory setting. For example, some demonstrations might be too dangerous, or too costly, to perform as a large-scale laboratory activity. Another reason for performing demonstrations is that it allows students to "see" a chemical reaction in a way that textbook graphics cannot depict. These demonstrations provide a visual framework for abstract concepts, facilitating the learning and understanding of this fundamental and central science discipline. "By using demonstrations in appropriate and thoughtful ways, teachers will teach better, inspire more, and increase the likelihood that chemistry will contribute to a better future for all of us." (Meyer, et al., 2003)

I have been using lecture demonstrations consistently during my first three years of teaching, but I find that my students still have negative feelings toward the subject of chemistry that I hold so dear. How can I better utilize demonstrations in a way that empowers my students' learning of high school chemistry? This was the question that fueled my personal inquiry into this matter.

Inquiry Design

I teach a total of seventy-one students dispersed among three general level high school chemistry classes. In seeking to answer my wonderings, I developed a month long curriculum that consisted of a discrepant event demonstration for each and every time my class met. Since my school is on a block schedule, my classes meet three times a week. A total of thirteen demonstrations were used in the teaching of this unit. These demonstrations explored the topics of acid and base chemistry, dynamic equilibrium, and catalysis. Most of the demonstrations came from handouts I had received from the chemical supply company, Flinn Scientific, while attending sessions at several National Science Teacher Association conferences. After the unit was over and all assessments were complete, the students began preparing demonstrations to perform for third, fourth, and fifth graders at an elementary school in our district. The instructional goals of these "shows" were for the high school students to gain a deeper understanding of the chemistry that was taking place in their demonstrations, and for the elementary students to understand the difference between a chemical and physical change.

My students were quizzed and tested prior to the Demo-a-Day unit to gauge their current levels of achievement in my chemistry class. During the unit, students videotaped me performing each of the thirteen demonstrations. Students were then quizzed and tested on the content of the Demo-a-Day unit. During these assessments, the videotapes were played back for the students to help stimulate their thought processes and remind them of what they had previously observed in class. Following this assessment, I then placed my students in groups of four. Each group selected one of the thirteen demonstrations that they had previously observed in the Demo-a-Day unit. Groups then prepared the necessary solutions, planned a script, and practiced their demonstrations in front of their peers. Students were asked to complete a demonstration show planning form, which I collected and graded. In this form, students had to describe all aspects of their demonstration. This included the chemicals they would need to use, the script they would use as they were performing the demonstration for the elementary school students, and the safety hazards of their specific demonstration. Groups were then videotaped as they performed their demonstration shows for the elementary students. Following the show, students were asked to write a reflective paper on both the Demo-a-Day unit and the demonstration show. Students also completed a Likert attitude assessment form. This consisted of ten items measuring student feelings toward chemistry, the Demo-a-Day unit, and the demonstration show.

During this entire unit, I reflected in my journal after each of the demonstrations was performed, and as I reviewed the videotapes. I then compared student grades before and after the unit, and used graphic organizers to compile my data. Student reflections were graded, and data obtained from the Likert attitude assessment was graphically represented on pie charts.

What I Learned

A number of claims can be made from this study. The first is that there appeared to be no correlation between the use of teacher demonstrations and achievement in my chemistry class. This was observed when grades before and after the demonstration unit were compared.

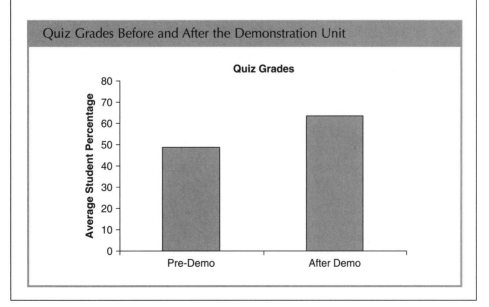

Quiz Grades Before and After the Demonstration Unit

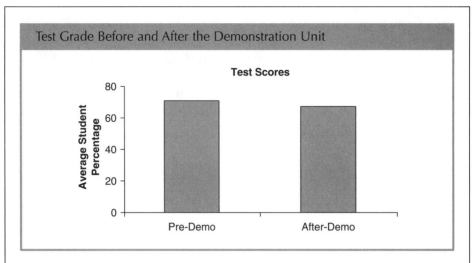

After careful examination of these graphs, it is apparent that no significant changes were observed in the achievement on my tests or quizzes in my class. While the average quiz grade increased, the test grades actually slightly decreased. This indicates to me that a number of factors need to be taken into consideration when assessing my students. First, I do not think that these grades can be directly attributed to the use of the demonstrations every day. They may be due to the amount of laboratory experiences in this unit, or to a more complex nature of the topics that were addressed in this unit. Second, perhaps students were not performing to their full potential due to a lack of motivation that often accompanies the start of the third quarter of the school year. Regardless of the causes, future research would need to be done to make claims about the use of demonstrations and the achievement in chemistry class.

My second claim from this inquiry is that students believe that both the Demo-a-Day unit and the demonstration show actually increased their understanding of chemistry. Regardless of the lack of significant improvement in test and quiz scores, students do feel like they learned something. I think that this could lead to better attitudes in my class. In turn, this might potentially challenge the self-fulfilling prophecy that "chemistry is impossible" that so many of my students seem to carry into class. The Likert attitude assessment, in particular, revealed this dimension of increased student efficacy.

Videotape evidence and examinations of student reflections revealed that students truly enjoyed the Demo-a-Day unit and the demonstration show. This leads to my third claim. The process used in this inquiry was enjoyable to both the high school students and to the elementary students who observed the demonstration show. High school students were heard in the videotapes enthusiastically expressing comments such as, "That's amazing," "I loved

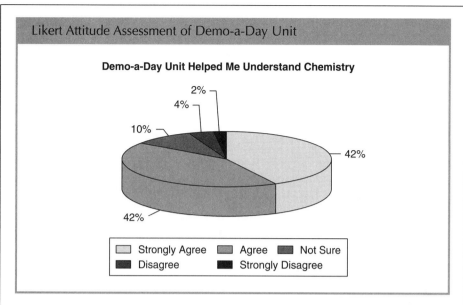

Likert Attitude Assessment of Demo-a-Day Unit

Demo-a-Day Unit Helped Me Understand Chemistry

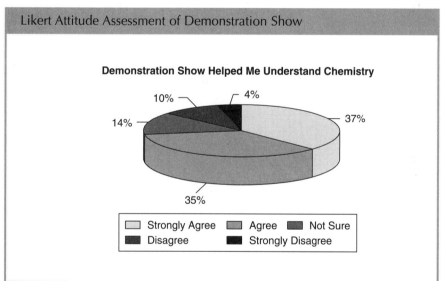

Likert Attitude Assessment of Demonstration Show

Demonstration Show Helped Me Understand Chemistry

that," and "That's what I am talking about!" In addition to these statements, the amount of engagement that I observed in the videotapes leads me to believe that the students were truly enjoying the demonstrations as a welcome change from a traditional lecture style. The elementary students also expressed their excitement. They, too, made statements following the demonstration show, such as, "Cool!" "Awesome!" and "That's neat." One elementary student even said, "I'm going to be a chemical scientist one day." Another asked, "Will I get to do that in high school?" One elementary teacher wrote, "I just wanted to take a minute to thank you, on behalf of the third grade team, for the awesome chemistry demonstration show last week. Our third graders really enjoyed the show and learned 'and saw' real-life chemical reactions." Based on these findings, claims can be made that student attitudes toward this unit and culminating show were very positive.

Reflections and Future Practice

Although no significant claims could be made regarding the achievement of my students being a result of daily teacher demonstrations, I feel confident concluding that the Demo-a-Day unit, coupled with the student-facilitated demonstration show, positively impacted student feelings in regard to the subject of chemistry, in general. As a teacher-researcher, this led me to recognize the profound significance of demonstrations in the high school chemistry classroom. It was revealed that demonstrations should not be the sole method of teaching chemistry, but should be supplemented with other hands-on experiences, such as laboratory investigations. I agree with Beall when he says, "Demonstrations are only one of many teaching techniques and should not be used for their own sake" (Beall, 1996, p. 641). However, demonstrations do lead to lasting memories and positive attitudes about the subject. Therefore, demonstrations should be encouraged at the high school level. Additionally, elementary students are impacted when high school students perform demonstrations for them. They learn beginning chemistry concepts while the high school students learn how to explain complex concepts in a simplified way. Both younger and older students are positively impacted. Based on my findings here, I plan to make the chemistry demonstration show an annual event.

Two important questions arose as a result of this study that I plan to examine in the future. First, what impact did *student* performances of the "exocharmic" demonstrations have on their own learning? At the time of this writing, students had not yet been tested following their show for the elementary students. Perhaps direct student planning and facilitation of demonstrations played a more significant role in their conceptual development and understanding than would have been possible by merely observing teacher-executed demonstrations. Another question to look into is whether or not the elementary students will truly remember the demonstrations in future years. If they do, will they enter my high school classroom with a better outlook on the subject of chemistry? Will they be better rooted in the fundamental concepts of chemistry than students who didn't witness demonstrations like these when they were in elementary school?

In closing I am going to list some of my favorite quotes from the student reflection assignment. They truly reveal the change in attitudes that occurred during my inquiry:

- "In the beginning I really didn't understand the reason behind the demonstration of the 'chemistry' of it. But when we actually had to mix our own chemicals and make the reaction happen, it made me understand everything a lot better."
- "The Demo-a-Day was a great and fun learning experience."
- "At that very moment, I wanted to be a chemistry teacher."
- "I think you should do this next year with the upcoming chemistry class. The demos were the most exciting thing we've done all year."
- "Things like this make Chemistry fun."

References

Beall, H. (1996). Demonstrations as a teaching tool in chemistry: Pro and con. *Journal of Chemical Education, 73*(7), 641.

Bodner, G. M. (2001). Why lecture demonstrations are 'exocharmic' for both students and their instructors. *U. Chem. Ed., 5,* 31–35.

Dana, N. F., & Yendol-Silva, D. (2003). *The reflective educator's guide to classroom research: Learning to teach and teaching to learn through practitioner inquiry.* Thousand Oaks, CA: Corwin Press.

Louters, L. L., & Huisman, R. D. (1999). Promoting chemistry at the elementary level: A low-maintenance program of chemical demonstrations. *Journal of Chemical Education, 76*(2), 196–198.

Meyer, L. S., Schmidt, S., Nozawa, F., Panee, D., & Kisler, M. (2003). Using demonstrations to promote student comprehension in chemistry. *Journal of Chemical Education, 80*(4), 431–435.

Thompson, J., & Soyibo, K. (2002) Effects of lecture, teacher demonstrations, discussion and practical work on 10th graders' attitudes to chemistry and understanding of electrolysis. *Research in Science & Technological Education, 20*(1), 25–37.

SAMPLE PROFESSIONAL DEVELOPMENT PLAN FORM

Name: **School:**   **Year:**
Inquiry Goal: **Inquiry Question:**
                                              Principal:

Connection of Inquiry to School Improvement Plan:

Needs of Children	Objectives (Refer to gain goals)	Activities and Resources Needed to Meet Objectives	Data Sources (How you will know if gains are being achieved?)	Criteria for Success (How will you know when objectives are met?)	Timeline for Completion

Initial Planning Conference	Interim Conference	Final Conference	Special Notes
Date: Comments:	Date: Comments:	Date: Goal Met? Yes ____ No ____ Comments:	This teacher consistently meets and/or exceeds the program's expected level of competency in the following areas: • Instruction • Student Performance • Class Management • Interpersonal Relations • Professional Responsibilities
What questions are being raised related to teacher and student learning?	Findings: Teacher and Student Learning	Findings: Teacher and Student Learning	Principal's Signature _____ Date _____

LAKE BUTLER SHOWCASE PROGRAM

LAKE BUTLER MIDDLE SCHOOL
ACTION RESEARCH PROJECTS

The four LBMS teachers listed below have participated in a year-long action research project in which they problematized their practice, systematically studied their practice, and took action for change based on their studies. This process illustrates educators taking charge of their own professional development. This is a shortened version of their presentation that will be held at P.K. Yonge Developmental Research School at the University of Florida on April 21.

Interest Is THE Center of Learning by Brian Tomlinson

After studying my students' grades and the frequency in which they were turning in homework, I discovered their interest in the material was declining as the year progressed. I decided that I needed to change the way I was presenting the material and started using centers. The centers allowed the students to be involved in teaching the material.

New Kids in the Block by April Crawford

In previous years, the fifth graders at my school have been on a typical middle school schedule of seven-period days. The fifth graders this year have been on a block schedule, having four teachers instead of the usual six teachers. Will the new block scheduling in fifth grade benefit the students, teachers, and parents?

So Much Time, So Little Experience: How Can Classroom Management for a New Teacher Be Effective Yet Productive? by Philip Marston

As a first-year fifth grade reading teacher, I immediately became concerned about how to be a good manager of time and resources. I needed to find out what motivates these young students to be and do their best. Through the process of trial and error, I am beginning to learn some things that work well, and some that don't. This has enabled me to adjust my own classroom behavior to help begin turning this wondering into fact.

Visualizing: It's Just Like Describing a Picture, Only Backwards! by Mark Freeland

Since I began teaching, I have asked my students about the pictures or movies they see in their minds as they read. At first

I was astonished by the number of kids that had no clue what I was talking about. I am hoping to gain some insight as to where the process breaks down and how to teach, coach, model, coax, or somehow help readers who do not visualize while reading to acquire this gift.

The following LBMS teachers are sharing best practices from their classroom:

Station Rotation by Gail Peacock

I needed to cover the main topics from two chapters in a short amount of time. I created folders for each of the main topics. Included in the folders were all the materials needed and the directions for completing the assignment at that station. The students had fifteen minutes at each station. The activities varied at each station, such as WEB construction from an article in a *Junior Scholastic*, Venn diagrams, and an Internet site to research. I took a class grade for each day to encourage completion at each station and then an open note quiz on the last day to get a grade for accuracy. The day after the stations were completed, we discussed the main ideas at each station.

Character Education Infusion Process by Will Bowen

With the dissolution of the traditional two-parent household, values and morals are not being assimilated to our youth. The six-step process allows important character traits such as honesty and respect to be taught by all teachers throughout all disciplines. Students can receive this necessary instruction by default rather than through a separate program. The six-step process and lesson plan examples will be provided.

Welcome to Study Island by Donna Harris

This presentation is a brief overlook of a Web-based program that allows students to master FCAT benchmarks. The program is teacher-friendly and the reports are crystal clear and breathtaking.

Accelerated Math by Priscilla Conner

This individual self-paced math program is being implemented in the math classes of LBMS. This program has proven to be great for struggling math students because it takes them from a level of success and then builds on that success. The assessment portion targets deficiencies, making it easy to track the progress of the students.

Parts of Speech by Julia Rooks

After introducing and working with adverbs and adjectives for several weeks, I found that my students were still having difficulty grasping the concepts. I knew that I needed to help them break the task into small bits and help them "see" the connections of each word. These two activities helped my students and made it less frustrating for me.

The Essential Question in the Classroom by Prudence Pate

As a review of all tested reading benchmarks for sixth grade, I involved the students by assigning groups to teach each benchmark. The students did a super job, but getting started was very difficult. We discovered that using the essential question for the specific benchmark helped the group focus on the skill and direct the planning and instruction. The lessons were then taught to their peers in the classroom. It not only increased the students' knowledge and understanding of the subject, but assisted me in *evaluating* their knowledge of the skills.

Interrogative Inclusion by
Mary Kay Metz and Rebecca Abercrombie

The inclusion classroom is something that is often misunderstood or even maligned until you have the honor of taking part in one. Like all new coteachers, we have stumbled and worried our way through the year, and have learned to use our strengths and weaknesses to cocreate and coteach units such as this one on the strategy QAR.

Customized (Lesson-Specific)
Graphic Organizers by Robert Ulmei

I noticed during several of the previous Wednesday afternoon sessions that many teachers were interested in increasing their use and variety of graphic organizers, but that most of the ideas directly employed the standard formats (KWLs, webs, 3-column notes, etc.). I often give my students customized graphic organizers that I have created for specific lessons, and the results are even greater than with the standard formats.

8th Graders Helping 6th Graders: A Cross-Age Tutoring Model by Nancy Griffis

As teachers, we all see the need to help students succeed in school. We also know that there are not enough hours in the day and that we often need more help to do our jobs properly. Using cross-age tutoring, I have found a way to get more people involved, therefore supplying more help to students. This one-onone tutoring situation is a win-win situation for everyone involved.

Rainforest Project by Glenda Gunter

This unit project was designed in my sixth grade classroom to encourage more independent reading on the topic of study. Students were to complete a poster linking together the location of rainforests, causes of damage to the rainforests, and effects of the damage. This "Quadrant D" project could be adapted to any subject area to make the students become actively involved in their learning.

Thanks to all teachers who presented today. Since we have the BEST teachers, we also have the BEST ideas. Hopefully, you have found some techniques or programs to use in your own classrooms. This shows the importance of sharing and collaborating as a faculty. You may think your ideas are simple, but someone else may be able to use them. Many of you have expressed a desire to visit the classrooms of your peers. Next year we are planning to create a schedule in which you will have a substitute for at least one day during the year for the purpose of visiting other classes at LBMS. This will enable you see the great things that are happening at our school and take ideas back to your own class.

7

From Good
to Great

*Lessons Learned in Coaching
an Inquiry-Oriented PLC*

The problem is not that we do not have enough good teachers. The problem is we have way too many. There is too much "good teaching." This good teaching has become totally acceptable, and some teachers have been doing a good job for years. Good has become marginalized. To create a major improvement in learning within a system or a district or even a state, we need programs that will move large numbers of good teachers to become great teachers. (Barkley, 2005, p. 20)

Coaching an inquiry-oriented professional development community assists good teachers in their quest to become great! The movement of teachers from good to great is heavily dependent on the coaching they receive. Yet, relatively few resources are available for coaches, staff developers, teacher-leaders, and principals that help make explicit the intricacies of coaching school-based professional development through the establishment of PLCs and engagement in action research. Hence, we believe that just as there exists too many good teachers, there exist too many good coaches. To tap into the power school-based professional development has to move good teachers, good students, and good schools to become great teachers, great students, and great schools, *good* coaches need to become *great* coaches! Good professional development coaches become great professional development coaches by looking deeply at the practice of coaching, connecting with and learning from others who engage in the act of coaching, and systematically studying their own coaching practice.

In the previous chapters of this book, we have looked deeply at some of the critical elements of establishing and facilitating an inquiry-oriented PLC, including building a healthy PLC (Chapter 2), helping PLC members develop a wondering (Chapter 3), helping PLC members develop a plan for their inquiries (Chapter 4), helping PLC members analyze data (Chapter 5), and helping PLC members share their work with others (Chapter 6). In an effort to connect you to others engaged in the act of coaching, in each one of these chapters, we drew on the experiences and stories of many of the talented coaches we have worked with throughout the years. We end this book by further connecting you to other professionals committed to coaching powerful professional development in their schools, as we briefly share twelve lessons learned from these coaches, as well as our own coaching practice.

ONE DOZEN LESSONS FOR COACHING INQUIRY-ORIENTED PLCs

Lesson #1: Start Small

An inquiry-oriented PLC works well with a group of six to twelve committed people. The larger the group, the more logistical nightmares can occur. By organizing the PLCs within your schools so that they don't grow beyond six to twelve participants, the group will have a better chance at establishing routines, meeting logistics, shared focus, inquiry stance, and relationships. These are key components needed to sustain collaboration focused on teacher learning. Coaches we have worked with from Broward and Alachua County in Florida have indicated that "starting small" within their school during the first year allowed them to build interest and commitment from the "bystanders" who were watching from afar. As a group of teacher-leaders, sometimes referred to as the pioneers, demonstrated the power and potential of collaborative learning to their colleagues, the reluctant teachers who had the chance to watch the PLC work unfold successfully joined the ranks of teacher-inquirers within their schools.

Lesson #2: Be Patient and Recognize That From Dissonance Comes Growth

Building a highly functioning, powerful inquiry-oriented PLC takes time. Additionally, the coach needs to be willing and prepared to work through initial struggles. Experienced coaches note that although the struggles will be many, growth always occurs out of the initial dissonance and discomfort. Coaches we have worked with have described the patience and challenges that they needed as they worked to create a trusting environment; help participants learn to serve as each other's critical friends; negotiate with school leaders for resources, time, and support; as well as shift participants' conception of professional development from a "sit and get" event to an inquiry-oriented process that requires changes in teaching practice and documentation of the results. The truth of the matter is that if you aren't feeling the need to exercise patience or noticing your PLC members experience a productive level of dissonance, you might want to revisit the essential elements of a healthy PLC described in Chapter 2.

Lesson #3: Be Flexible

Finding a time to meet can be one of the most challenging aspects of coaching a PLC. One coach we worked with, Jack Hughes, reflected that "Scheduling around school and family demands for our PLC work equates to tiptoeing through tulips (or minefields)." Similarly, after her first year of establishing and coaching a cross-district PLC to support teachers in her district as they engaged in action research for the first time, Debbi Hubbell reflects:

> "Being flexible" is the big lesson I learned from coaching this year . . . flexible with scheduling, with personalities, and with creative assistance. When our group first met, scheduling teachers from all over the county to meet on a day that there were no meetings was nearly impossible. One teacher had a college class on Mondays and Fridays, ran the afterschool program on Tuesdays and Thursdays, and had faculty meetings on Wednesdays. I wanted to say, "Why are you doing this also?" but realized that she was totally committed to learning about inquiry and was determined to help her faculty all become involved with it as well, so I decided it was worth my time to be creative with helping her. While she didn't always meet with our group, we worked out a schedule where I met with her during lunch or after her meetings and we did a lot of e-mailing. When she needed to miss our PDC

meetings, the others missed her input, but I kept them informed of what she was doing, and served as a "proxy," representing her work at our meetings, and delivering feedback to her from the group. Was it optimal? No. Yet, rather than excluding her, we made a commitment to work around her schedule when possible and use alternative plans when necessary. By being flexible, we all benefited greatly from her membership in our group, and perhaps more importantly, her school and students benefited as well.

Lesson #4: Involve the Principal

Principal support beyond simple approval is critical for the health of your PLC. View a part of your coaching role as educating and informing administration. Keep your principal abreast of the work of your PLC. Place articles about learning communities and action research in your principal's mailbox. Enlist your principal as a co-problem-poser and problem-solver to attack logistical issues such as when and where to meet and how to share the PLC work with other professionals in the school. If it's okay with PLC members, invite the principal to key meetings your group has during the year. A coach we know invited her administrator, who was not overly knowledgeable and supportive of the PLC work, to a meeting focused on data analysis that used the data analysis protocol described in Chapter 5. She reported that the principal was literally "blown away" by the quality of the dialogue that ensued among the teachers about their data, and subsequently, the principal became much more open to supporting the work of the PLC.

Lesson #5: Use the Protocols, but Don't Let the Protocols Use You!

Because the dialogue and conversation that occurs in education has not been structured traditionally, teachers have had few opportunities to engage in rich professional exchanges with their teaching colleagues. When teachers experience dialogue and conversation that is structured by the use of a protocol, like the principal who observed the data analysis meeting, they are often "blown away" by the richness of their exchange with colleagues. This rich exchange fills an empty void in the teacher's practice that has existed for years, and PLC members express how marvelous a protocol-led discussion has been for their professional learning.

Protocols *can* be very powerful, and are a wonderful coaching tool. However, the power of protocols can become seductive to coaches, when

PLC members marvel at how incredible the experience of engaging in dialogue using the protocol has been for them. This can lead some coaches to believe that the selection and teaching of protocols are the most important part of their coaching work. Coaches begin planning their PLC meetings around the question, "What protocol would be good for our PLC to try this week?" rather than "What is the next step in our collective work to move us closer to our PLC goals?" It's important to remember that the value of protocols is not in the protocols themselves, but in their ability to be used by you as a tool to move the PLC group members' collective work forward.

Lesson #6: Front Load Your Support—Start Early and Spend Time on the Wondering Development

---

Many coaches we have worked with realize after they have taken a group through an entire school year, they wish they had started earlier in the school year and spent some more time up front helping PLC group members define a wondering rather than moving quickly onto the next steps in the action research process so it felt like the group was making progress, as the school year was "ticking away." After her first year of coaching an inquiry-oriented learning community, Coach Joan Thate reflected that if she were to do it all over again, "I would push harder when I thought a question was not clearly enough defined or when it seemed to be a not very productive question."

Lesson #7: Provide Both Pressure and Support

"Pushing harder" is probably one of the most difficult aspects of being a coach. Coaches are sometimes afraid that pushing harder, or exerting some pressure on the thinking of a PLC member, could lead to conflict, or worse yet, a PLC member resigning from the group.

In general, it is much easier for a coach to provide support, and become a cheerleader and advocate for teachers, rather than exerting pressure on the teacher to delve deeper into his or her own thinking. Providing support and as one coach we worked with put it, "providing plenty of pats on the back" is an essential component of coaching and should not be taken for granted. Teaching and inquiring into teaching is incredible intense and difficult work. All PLC members need affirmation that their work as a teacher and member of the PLC is both valued and valuable.

Yet, support without pressure risks teachers feeling good about their practice without looking at that practice in new and different ways, and making improvements in practice that will enhance teaching and learning.

As a coach, providing support without pressure could ultimately lead toward a PLC going through all of motions of inquiry-oriented PLCs without rich, deep growth and development of PLC group members. All members of the PLC may be happy and feel good about themselves, but not learn and change as a result of the PLC work. The PLC work might run smoothly and look good from the outside-in, but become shallow and hollow when looked at from the inside-out. Outstanding coaches know that providing some pressure is a critical part of the teacher professional development equation: Pressure + Support = Teacher Learning and Change.

Lesson #8: Be Willing to Cause Discomfort

Sometimes pressure comes just by being willing to create some discomfort within your PLC. According to Barkley (2005):

> Coaching can move good teachers to become great teachers. It provides the strongest return on the investment of teaching. Coaches may cause discomfort at times. However, great coaches create environments where the coachee is comfortable with discomfort. Discomfort is key to growth and change. When good teachers become uncomfortable, that discomfort gives them impetus to improve, to wake up and get out of their box; it stimulates positive change. (p. 21)

Lesson #9: Be Wary of Mandated Participation

Sometimes pressure and discomfort comes from administration that mandates PLC work and/or action research. This creates an interesting dilemma for the coach. On the one hand, mandated participation might be the pressure an individual needs to become involved and a skilled coach can capitalize on that pressure and cultivate a commitment to PLC work in a member who originally started because it was mandated by the principal or district. On the other hand, mandated participation can also be an oxymoron. Engagement in an inquiry-oriented PLC requires that each individual PLC member make a commitment to look deeply and systematically at student learning as well as one's own teaching. Without that commitment, PLC work cannot succeed. So, which comes first, involvement or commitment? A skilled coach knows that voluntary participation in this professional development process is best, but simultaneously works with administration to reframe mandates as opportunities, and spread the growth of PLCs.

Lesson #10: Remember—Relationships Are Everything!

Every single coach we have worked with cites the relationships he or she developed with PLC members, and the PLC members develop with one another, as a primary factor associated with the success of the PLC work. Some coaches even attribute their bringing of food to early PLC meetings as an entrée into developing good relationships among the group's membership. One coach we worked with this year, Sherri Jackson, reflected, "The camaraderie of my PLC was wonderful. I did not feel like I was in charge, but that we were all in this together." Cultivating the feeling that "we're all in this together" is an essential part of the coaching process.

Lesson #11: Study Your Own Coaching Practice!

One way to create the feeling of "we're all in this together" is by engaging in systematic study of PLCs, the process of action research, and/or your own coaching practice, right alongside members of your PLC as they study their own classroom practices. For example, we learned a great deal about coaching PLCs and action research by using the action research process to study our own work with teachers. Early in our own action research work, we wished to transfer what we knew about teacher professional development to student-teacher supervision. We obtained permission to engage three student-teachers in a pilot program to reconceptualize the traditional student teaching seminar as an inquiry-oriented PLC. We met weekly with these student-teachers, and ran our sessions similarly to the ways we've outlined in this book. As the student-teachers were engaging in action research, we engaged in our own action research study to understand how they experienced the process of action research as preservice teachers (Dana & Silva, 2001). This inquiry laid the foundation for teachers' engagement in action research becoming a signature feature in the establishment of professional development schools at Penn State, our institution at the time (see, e.g., Dana & Silva, 2002; Dana, Silva, & Snow-Gerono, 2002; Silva & Dana, 2004). In another inquiry, as we coached a PLC and the members of our PLC were analyzing their data, we taught PLC members the data analysis process by analyzing the wonderings generated by teachers we had worked with over time as they engaged in action research (Dana et al., 2006). Finally, we recently engaged in an inquiry as members of the PLC we were coaching to examine our own practice as coaches of inquiry (Dana & Yendol-Hoppey, 2006). It was the data that we collected during this particular inquiry that led us to articulate the critical junctures in coaching an inquiry-oriented PLC, and ultimately, led to the writing of this book!

Other coaches we know that have studied aspects of their own coaching practice, PLCs, and/or action research alongside of teachers they were coaching in an inquiry-oriented PLC include Debbi Hubbell (2006), who explored how to best utilize her time in her new position of reading coach; Kim Sullivan (2006), who studied the positive impact a critical friends group had on the teaching practices of group members; Mickey McDonald and Gloria Weber (2007), who explored using PLCs to initiate schoolwide knowledge of differentiated instruction and how it might play out at the secondary level; Greg Cunningham (2007), who investigated how he could minimize the negative effects of his absenteeism from class due to the responsibilities he was taking on as a teacher-leader at his school; and Jack Hughes (2007), who examined the effects on his school's culture when a first-time, schoolwide action research project was instituted. Engaging in your own inquiry as you coach others in the inquiry process and making your own inquiry transparent to the group members you are coaching is not only a wonderful way to create a "we're all in this together" atmosphere, but to improve your own coaching practice and serve as a model for your PLC members as well!

Lesson #12: Remember: It's the Journey, Not the Destination!

Once you've coached your PLC through one cycle of inquiry, at the end of the school year, it may feel like your work is complete . . . and yet, you can clearly see that so much more work lies ahead. It is easy for coaches to become discouraged, and even wonder if the intense work of coaching is worth it!

At this point, it's important to remember that teaching and learning are incredibly complex endeavors. One of the most wonderful aspects of inquiry-oriented PLC work is that it is a form of professional development that honors all the great complexity that is inherent in teaching. For this reason, engaging in inquiry and coaching school-based professional development is not about solving every educational problem that exists—it's about finding new and better problems to study, and in so doing, leading a continuous cycle of self and school improvement...truly, becoming the best that you can be and helping others to become their best as well. Remember that your work as a coach is about living this journey, not reaching one particular destination.

Your journey as a coach of school-based professional development is of critical importance to keeping teachers, students, and schools alive! We believe no other author captures the importance of coaching teacher learning than Roland Barth (1981) in the following quote we used at the very opening of this book. Coming full circle, we end this book as we began it:

Nothing within a school has more impact upon students in terms of skills development, self-confidence, or classroom behavior than the personal and professional growth of their teachers. When teachers examine, question, reflect on their ideas and develop new practices that lead towards their ideals, students are alive. When teachers stop growing, so do their students. (Barth, 1981, p. 145)

Through coaching, you breathe new life into teachers. You breathe new life into teaching. You touch the lives of countless students you will never even meet—the students of the teachers you coach. For them, you keep learning alive. For them, continue on your coaching journey!

References

Adams, A., Boynton, S., Church, L., & Gould, C. (Eds.). (2007). *Improving Immokalee schools through teacher inquiry: Proceedings from the 2006 Immokalee inquiry expo.* Gainesville, FL: Lastinger Center for Learning.

Barkley, S. G. (2005). *Quality teaching in a culture of coaching.* Lanham, MD: Scarecrow Education.

Barth, R. (1981). The principal as staff developer. *Journal of Education, 163*(2), 144–162.

Barth, R. (2006). Improving relationships within the schoolhouse. *Educational Leadership, 63*(6), 8–13.

Barth, R. S. (1990). *Improving schools from within: Teachers, parents, and principals can make the difference.* San Francisco: Jossey-Bass.

Beyer, T. (2007, April). *Reading habits of high school seniors.* Presentation at the third annual Teaching, Inquiry, and Innovation Showcase, Gainesville, FL.

Brandenburg, J., & Yendol-Hoppey, D. (2007). *Everybody wants to improve but not everybody wants to change: One school's story of using teacher inquiry to improve instruction.* Unpublished manuscript.

Bryk, A., & Schneider, B. (2002). *Trust in schools: A core resource for improvement.* New York: Russell Sage Foundation.

Burgin, S. (2007). A demo-a-day in high school chemistry. In N. F. Dana & D. C. Delane (Eds.), *Improving Florida schools through teacher inquiry: Selections from the 2006 teaching, inquiry, and innovation showcase* (pp. 126–133). Gainesville, FL: Center for School Improvement.

Caro-Bruce, C., Flessner, R., Klehr, M., & Zeichner, K. M. (2007). *Creating equitable classrooms through action research.* Thousand Oaks, CA: Corwin Press.

Caro-Bruce, C., & McCreadie, J. (1994). Establishing action research in one school district. In S. Noffke (Ed.), *Practically critical: An invitation to action research in education* (pp. 33–40). New York: Teachers College Press.

Carr, W., & Kemmis, S. (1986). *Becoming critical: Education, knowledge and action research.* Geelong, Victoria, Australia: Deakin University Press.

Cochran-Smith, M., & Lytle, S. L. (1993). *Inside/outside: Teacher research and knowledge.* New York: Teachers College Press.

Cochran-Smith, M., & Lytle, S. L. (1999a). Relationships of knowledge and practice: Teacher learning in communities. *Review of Research in Education, 24,* 249–305.

Cochran-Smith, M., & Lytle, S. L. (1999b). The teacher research movement: A decade later. *Educational Researcher, 28*(7), 15–25.

Cochran-Smith, M., & Lytle, S. L. (2001). Beyond certainty: Taking an inquiry stance on practice. In A. Lieberman & L. Miller (Eds.), *Teachers caught in the action: Professional development that matters* (pp. 45–58). New York: Teachers College Press.

Creswell, J. W. (2002). *Qualitative inquiry and research design.* Thousand Oaks, CA: SAGE.

Cunningham, G. (2007, April). *Good teachers gone . . . bad: How can I minimize the negative effects of "teacher-leader" absenteeism?* Paper presented at the third annual Teaching, Inquiry, and Innovation Showcase, Gainesville, FL.

Cushman, K. (1999). The cycle of inquiry and action: Essential learning communities. *Horace, 15*(4). Retrieved November 12, 2007, from http://www.essentialschools.org/cs/resources/view/ces_res/74

Dana, N. F., & Baker, J. (Eds.). (2006). *Improving Florida schools through teacher inquiry: Selections from the 2005 teaching, inquiry, and innovation showcase.* Gainesville: Center for School Improvement and North East Florida Educational Consortium.

Dana, N. F., & Delane, D. C. (Eds.). (2007). *Improving Florida schools through teacher inquiry: Selections from the 2006 teaching, inquiry, and innovation showcase.* Gainesville: Center for School Improvement and North East Florida Educational Consortium.

Dana, N. F., & Silva, D. Y. (2001). Student teachers as researchers: Developing an inquiry stance towards teaching. In J. Rainer & E. M. Guyton (Eds.), *Research on the effects of teacher education on teacher performance: Teacher education yearbook IX* (pp. 94–104). New York: Kendall-Hunt.

Dana, N. F., & Silva, D. Y. (2002). Building an inquiry-oriented PDS: Inquiry as a part of mentor teacher work. In I. N. Guadarrama, J. Nath, & J. Ramsey (Eds.), *Forging alliances in community and thought: Research in professional development schools* (pp. 87–104). Greenwich, CT: Information Age.

Dana, N. F., Silva, D. Y., & Snow-Gerono, J. (2002). Building a culture of inquiry in professional development schools. *Teacher Education and Practice, 15*(4), 71–89.

Dana, N. F., & Yendol-Hoppey, D. (2006, April). *Facilitating the inquiry of others.* Paper presented at the second annual Teaching, Inquiry, and Innovation Showcase, Gainesville, FL.

Dana, N. F., Yendol-Hoppey, D., & Snow-Gerono, J. L. (2006). Deconstructing inquiry in the professional development school: Exploring the domains and contents of teachers' questions. *Action on Teacher Education, 27*(4), 59–71.

Dana, N. F., & Yendol-Silva, D. (2003). *The reflective educator's guide to classroom research: Learning to teach and teaching to learn through practitioner inquiry.* Thousand Oaks, CA: Corwin Press.

Darling-Hammond, L., & McLaughlin, M. W. (1995). Policies that support professional development in an era of reform. *Phi Delta Kappan, 76*(8), 597–604.

Dempsie, G. (1997). Using puppets in a primary classroom: A teacher-researcher's findings. *Teaching and Learning: The Journal of Natural Inquiry, 11*(3), 5–13.

Dempsie, G. (2000). Can I love you? A child's adventure with puppets and play. *The Journal of Imagination in Language Learning, 5,* 28–36.

Dillon, P. W. (2007). *Policies to enable teacher collaboration.* Retrieved November 12, 2007, from http://www.teachersnetwork.org/tnli/research/growth/dillon.htm

Drennon, C. E., & Cervero, R. M. (2002). The politics of facilitation: Negotiating power and politics in practitioner inquiry groups. *Adult Education Quarterly, 52,* 193–209.

DuFour, R. (1999). Challenging role: Playing the part of principal stretches one's talent. *Journal of Staff Development, 20*(4), 62–63.

DuFour, R. (2004). What is a "professional learning community?" *Educational Leadership, 61*(8), 6–11.

DuFour, R., & Eaker, R. (1998). *Professional learning communities at work: Best practices for enhancing student achievement.* Bloomington, IN: National Educational Service.

Easton, L. B. (2004). *Powerful designs for professional learning.* Oxford, OH: National Staff Development Council.

Emm, L. (2007). *Protocols in practice: A passionate inquiry into teacher practice.* Retrieved on June 19, 2007, from http://www.harmonyschool.org/nsrf/connections_auth_arch.html

Fullan, M. (1999). *Change forces: The sequel.* Philadelphia: Falmer.

Fullan, M. (2001). *Leading in a culture of change.* San Francisco: Jossey-Bass.

Fullan, M. G., & Miles, M. B. (1995). Getting reform right. In A. C. Ornstein & L. S. Behar (Eds.), *Contemporary issues in curriculum* (pp. 403–414). Boston: Allyn & Bacon.

Garmston, R. J. (2007). Results-oriented agendas transform meetings into valuable collaborative events. *Journal of Staff Development Council, 28*(2), 55–56.

Gay, G. (2000). *Culturally responsive teaching: Theory, research, & practice.* New York: Teachers College Press.

Glaser, B. (1978). *Theoretical sensitivity: Advances in the methodology of grounded theory.* Mill Valley, CA: Sociology Press.

Hargreaves, A. (1994). *Changing teachers, changing times: Teachers' work and culture in the postmodern age.* New York: Teachers College Press.

Hubbard, R. S., & Power, B. M. (1999). *Living the questions: A guide for teacher researchers.* York, ME: Stenhouse.

Hubbell, D. (2005, April). *Focus on fractured fairy tales and fluency flourishes.* Presentation at the Teaching, Inquiry, and Innovation Showcase, Gainesville, FL.

Hubbell, D. (2006). New reading coach: How can I best utilize my time and activities? In N. F. Dana & D. C. Delane (Eds.), *Improving Florida schools through teacher inquiry: Selections from the 2006 teaching, inquiry and innovation showcase.* Gainesville, FL: Center for School Improvement.

Hughes, J. (2007, April). *Schoolwide action research (a new beginning of wonderings).* Paper presented at the third annual Teaching, Inquiry, and Innovation Showcase, Gainesville, FL.

Hunter, D., Bailey, A., & Taylor, B. (1995). *The zen of groups: A handbook for people meeting with a purpose.* Tucson, AZ: Fisher Books.

Jacobs, J. (2007). *Coaching for equity: The transformation of field supervisors' pedagogy in a professional learning community.* Doctoral dissertation, University of Florida, Gainesville.

Johnson, S. (1998). *Who moved my cheese?* New York: Putnam.

Killion, J., & Harrison, C. (2006). *Taking the lead: New roles for teachers and school-based coaches.* Oxford, OH: National Staff Development Council.

Kincheloe, J. (1991). *Teachers as researchers: Qualitative inquiry as a path to empowerment.* London: Falmer.

Kruse, S., Louis, K. S., & Bryk, A. (1994). *Building professional community in schools: Issues in restructuring, center on organization and restructuring of schools.* Madison: Wisconsin Center for Education Research, University of Wisconsin–Madison.

Lambert, L., Collay, M., Dietz, M. E., Kent, K., & Richert, A. E. (1996). *Who will save our schools? Teachers as constructivist leaders.* Thousand Oaks, CA: Corwin Press.

Little, J. W. (1981). *School success and staff development in urban desegregated schools: A summary of recently completed research.* Boulder, CO: Center for Action Research.

Luekens, M. T., Lyter, D. M., Fox, E. E., & Chandler, K. (2004). *Teacher attrition and mobility: Results from the teacher follow-up survey, 2000–01* (NCES 2004–301). Washington, DC: National Center for Educational Statistics, U.S. Department of Education.

Masingila, J. O. (2006). *Teachers engaged in research: Inquiry into mathematics classrooms, grades 3–5.* Greenwich, CT: Information Age Publishing.

McDonald, J. P., Mohr, N., Dichter, A., & McDonald, E. C. (2003). *The power of protocols: An educator's guide to better practice.* New York: Teachers College Press.

McDonald, M., & Weber, G. (2007, April). *Using professional learning communities to initiate school-wide practice and change.* Paper presented at the third annual Teaching, Inquiry, and Innovation Showcase, Gainesville, FL.

Meyers, E., & Rust, F. (Eds.). (2003). *Taking action with teacher research.* Portsmouth, NH: Heinemann.

Mills, G. E. (2003). *Action research: A guide for the teacher researcher.* Saddle River, NJ: Pearson Education.

National School Reform Faculty. (2007). *NSRF mission.* Retrieved June 19, 2007, from http://www.harmonyschool.org/nsrf/default.html

Patton, M. Q. (2000). *Qualitative research & evaluation methods* (3rd ed.). Thousand Oaks, CA: SAGE.

Roberts, S. M., & Pruitt, E. Z. (2003). *Schools as professional learning communities.* Thousand Oaks, CA: Corwin Press.

Ruddock, J., & Hopkins, D. (Eds.). (1985). *Research as a basis for teaching: Readings from the work of Lawrence Stenhouse.* London: Heinemann.

Schwandt, T. A. (1997). *Qualitative inquiry: A dictionary of terms.* Thousand Oaks, CA: SAGE.

Senge, P. (1990). *The fifth discipline: The art and practice of the learning organization.* New York: Doubleday.

Senge, P. (2007). *Skills and capabilities.* Retrieved November 11, 2007, from http://www.solonline.org/pra/tool/skills.html

Sergiovanni, T. (1994). *Building community in schools.* San Francisco: Jossey-Bass.

Sherman, R. R., & Webb, R. B. (1997). *Qualitative research in education: Focus and methods.* Philadelphia: Falmer.

Silva, D. Y., & Dana, N. F. (2004). Encountering new spaces: Teachers developing voice within a professional development school. *Journal of Teacher Education, 55*(2), 128–140.

Sullivan, K. (2006, April). *Help! Critical friends needed!* Paper presented at the second annual Teaching, Inquiry, and Innovation Showcase, Gainesville, FL.

Taylor, R. (2002). Shaping the culture of learning communities. *Principal Leadership, 3*(4), 42–45.

Teacher Leaders Network. (2007). *What issues do expert teachers and teacher coaches face when they are "inserted" into high-need schools?* Retrieved on June 13, 2007, from http://www.teacherleaders.org/old_site/Conversations/HTS/inserted_HTS.html

Whitford, B. L., & Wood, D. (in press). *Teachers learning in community: Realities and possibilities.* Albany: State University of New York Press.

Index